D0554845

This book is for our parents, who made a leap of faith and allowed two boys to travel like men; for the friends who traveled with us; for the photographers who inspired us; and for the railroaders who made us feel at home.

MAGNETIC NORTH
CANADIAN STEAM IN TWILIGHT

ROGER COOK & KARL ZIMMERMANN

WITH ADDITIONAL PHOTOGRAPHS BY JIM SHAUGHNESSY, DON WOOD AND OTHERS

The BOSTON
MILLS PRESS

Cataloguing in Publication Data
Cook, Roger, 1942-
Zimmermann, Karl, 1943-
Magnetic north: Canadian steam in twilight
Includes biographical references.
ISBN 1-55046-306-3

1. Railroads – Canada – History.
I. Zimmermann, Karl R. II. Title

TF26.C66 1999   385'.0971'09045
C99-931865-9

Copyright © Roger Cook & Karl Zimmermann,
1999. All rights reserved.

03 02 01 00 99   1 2 3 4 5

Published in 1999 by
Boston Mills Press
132 Main Street, Erin, Ontario
Canada N0B 1T0
Tel: (519) 833-2407   Fax: (519) 833-2195
e-mail: books@boston-mills.on.ca
www.boston-mills.on.ca

An affiliate of
Stoddart Publishing Co. Limited
34 Lesmill Road, Toronto, Ontario
Canada M3B 2T6
Tel: (416) 445-3333   Fax: (416) 445-5967
e-mail: gdsinc@genpub.com

Distributed in Canada by
General Distribution Services Ltd.
325 Humber College Blvd, Toronto,
Canada M9W 7C3
Orders: 1-800-387-0141 Ontario & Quebec
Orders: 1-800-387-0172 NW Ontario &
Other Provinces
customer.service@ccmail.gw.genpub.com
EDI Canadian Telebook S1150391

Distributed in the United States by
General Distribution Services Inc.
85 River Rock Drive, Suite 202
Buffalo, New York 14207-2170
Toll-free: 1-800-805-1083
Toll-free fax: 1-800-481-6207
e-mail: gdsinc@genpub.com
www.genpub.com
PUBNET 6307949

Text and cover design by
Chris McCorkindale and Sue Breen
McCorkindale Advertising & Design

Printed in Canada

Canada

THE CANADA COUNCIL | LE CONSEIL DES ARTS
FOR THE ARTS | DU CANADA
SINCE 1957 | DEPUIS 1957

*We acknowledge for their financial support of our publishing
program the Canada Council, the Ontario Arts Council, and
the Government of Canada through the Book Publishing
Industry Development Program (BPIDP).*

"Farewell to Canadian Steam" first appeared in
somewhat different form in *Trains* Magazine.

Cover photo
Two Pacifics in Montreal commuter service—G5
No. 1201 and G3 No. 2408—spend the night
at Vaudreuil in December 1959.
Karl Zimmermann

Rear jacket photo
Royal Hudson at St. Luc in Montreal,
December 1959. Roger Cook

Page 1
At Palmerston, Ontario, Train 179 waits to depart
for Southampton behind Ten-Wheeler No. 1348,
with diesel-powered Kincardine-bound Train 177
in the background. Jim Shaughnessy

Page 2
Toronto-bound Train 93 on the
Uxbridge Subdivision. Don Wood

Page 3
G2 No. 2527 at Vallée Jonction, Quebec.
Jim Shaughnessy

Page 5
Extra 5329 West is on the move after meeting
an eastbound at Birchton, Quebec.
Jim Shaughnessy

CONTENTS

Introduction
The Lure of Canadian Steam   7

Chapter 1
When Steam Ruled Montreal's
Suburban Services   11

Chapter 2
Last Citadel of Canadian National Steam   39

Chapter 3
Branch Line Canada   71

Chapter 4
Steam in Snow   99

Chapter 5
Farewell to Canadian Steam   127

Epilogue
Steam Lives On   145

Acknowledgments & Bibliography   160

THE LURE OF CANADIAN STEAM

*T*oday, from the far side of middle age, as if through a telescope held backwards, we look at our younger selves. It was the spring of 1958, and two boys, neighbors in the small New Jersey town of Oradell, planned for their upcoming trip to Montreal in different ways. The younger—he was 15—took the crisp ten-dollar bills that he received as an allowance and, rather than spending them on baseball cards or chocolate egg creams, stashed them in the front of his desk drawer, watching them accumulate until there were enough to cover his share of a double bedroom from New York to Montreal and back on the overnight *Montrealer/Washingtonian*, plus two nights in Montreal. Each week, when he slipped another bill on top of the tidy stack, he'd think about the substantial fleet of steam locomotives, both Canadian Pacific and Canadian National, still in service in Montreal and how he and his friend from across the street would travel north to see and photograph them. The previous summer, on a trip to Europe, his parents had given him a Zeiss-Ikon 35-millimeter camera, so he was ready.

Almost every day he pulled his favorite book, *The Age of Steam*, by Lucius Beebe and Charles Clegg, from the bottom shelf of his bookcase and thumbed through it, admiring the work of such great photographers as Jim Shaughnessy , Robert Hale, Richard Steinheimer, and Don Wood. In particular, Shaughnessy's

sparkling after-dark images of Canadian locomotives kept grabbing his attention. He'd never forget the particular heft and feel of this volume, the richness of the rotogravure printing, the peculiar smell of the paper. Forever onward, the florid excesses of Beebe's inimitable and somehow enchanting prose would seem the proper idiom for chronicling steam railroading.

Meanwhile, across the street, the senior member of the team (by a year) was also leafing through *The Age of Steam* and planning. He'd already had some first-hand experience with Canadian steam; now that he'd replaced his box camera with a 35-millimeter, he was anxious to get back north.

In the summer of 1956, he and his family had made a motor trip into Quebec, stopping to see the Central Vermont Railway at St. Albans. There, a Canadian National Pacific had been under steam, and one of CV's imposing 2-10-4's had been stored beside the shops. They'd continued on to Quebec City, staying at the Chateau Frontenac, the great Canadian Pacific hotel that towers medievally over the St. Lawrence River as it sweeps by the city. At nearby Palais Station, he and his dad had watched a Canadian Pacific 2-8-0 shuffling coaches and had spotted one of Canadian National's light Pacifics.

But it had been at La Malbaie, 88 miles east of Quebec City, on the St. Lawrence, that the bug had really bitten. The family had

Brockville, Ontario *Jim Shaughnessy*

stayed at the Manoir Richelieu, a stone castle on a hill that looked conveniently down on the Canadian National tracks. It was at the base of this parapet that a way freight, powered by light Pacific No. 5049, sadly in need of some cosmetic attention (paint, or at least water), had stalled on fog-dampened rails. The boy, sans camera, had watched and listened as the Pacific tried again and again to restart its train. Each time the 69-inch drivers slipped, towering clouds of exhaust billowed upward to partially obscure the drama below and rain cinders on the spectator above. Eventually, the engineer reversed direction and backed out of sight; then, with sharp barks of rapidly increasing exhaust, the way freight stormed back, this time with a good roll on, and worked steadily upgrade and off into the distance, until nothing remained to mark its passing but a lingering smudge of fragrant coal smoke and the muted beat of exhaust.

Later, with the train tied up at the small yard in La Malbaie, and 5049 balanced on the "armstrong" turntable, the conductor (from the Ukraine, and therefore a self-styled "Ukrainian Canadian") had lifted the heavy kerosene markers off their brackets and stowed them, then invited the boy and his father aboard his caboose, or van, as these cars were universally known in Canada. It was high-cupolaed, wooden, painted Morency orange and splashed with Canadian National's showy maple-leaf logo. This welcome would prove to be entirely typical of the warm hospitality of Canadian railroaders that the boys would encounter in the years just ahead.

Then the passenger train from Quebec City had pulled into the La Malbaie station behind another light Pacific, No. 5077, the same class as its dowdy, dusty sister from the way freight, but another kettle of fish entirely. Driver tires were striped in white. Boiler was wiped to a lustrous sheen. Beetle-browed with an

La Malbaie.

Both photos: Roger Cook

Quebec City train at La Malbaie.

8

Elesco feedwater heater, it had seemed to be wearing a crown—a regal, stately presence, surely, even haughty. The young photographer had checked the timetable and was certain to have his camera ready this time.

Baggage was still being heaped on carts when he and his dad drove off, heading up the hill to dinner at Manoir Richelieu. The next day the family was off to Tadoussac, where they put their car aboard the steamer *St. Lawrence* for a voyage up the Saguenay River to Chicoutimi. From there they began the return journey home, a journey on which the boy carried with him some tantalizing visions of steam railroading in Canada.

With armstrong turntable, bucket coaling station, and two-stall enginehouse, La Malbaie reeked of small-time, steam-powered style; it was the epitome of old-fashioned railroading, still rich in humanity. It was labor-intensive to a fault, with stations sprouting train-order boards (and, inside, the operators or station agents to set them) and engine terminals where locomotives sometimes were turned by men with strong backs as well as strong arms, and sometimes were fueled using derricks to wrestle hulking buckets to tender-top. If labor-intensive, it was also irresistible.

The centerpiece, of course, was the steam locomotive, with its rich array of required facilities and attendants. As young boys had for many generations, we two from Oradell had already fallen under the spell of those charismatic machines. In the late summer and fall of 1957, we had caught a glimpse of Pennsylvania Railroad's K4's (and less famous brethren) running their last miles. In December, we'd journeyed to Roanoke to photograph the high-powered modern steam of the Norfolk & Western Railway. Now, piqued by images in *The Age of Steam* and coverage by David Morgan and Philip Hastings in *Trains* Magazine, as well as the personal recollections of one, we looked north.

On May 29, 1958, after dinner with our families, we stood amid the soon-to-be-razed classical grandeur of New York's incomparable Pennsylvania Station, ready to board the *Montrealer* for our first trip together to Canada in search of steam. In the next two years we'd return frequently—by train at first and, later, by car. We'd venture often to Montreal, and also to Toronto, to the Waltham Branch running west from Ottawa, and finally to Quebec's Eastern Townships to witness steam's very last stand on the Canadian Pacific main line to the Atlantic Provinces. Some places—like Chipman, home of the legendary 4-4-0's—we'd learn of, yearn for, but never get a chance to visit.

We'd encounter (and sometimes travel with) others who enriched our understanding of Canadian railroading. Eventually we'd meet some of the photographers—Don Wood and Jim Shaughnessy, in particular—whose work we'd pored over with such admiration in *The Age of Steam* and in the magazines. What follows is a record of our travels, some armchair but mostly real, into Canada in those magic days when steam still ran—when the air was sweet with hot grease and sour with coal smoke, when cinders crunched under foot, and when the crack of locomotive exhaust echoed off the hills.

The *Washingtonian* at St. Albans.

Jim Shaughnessy

WHEN STEAM RULED MONTREAL'S SUBURBAN SERVICES

Standing trackside on the Canadian Pacific's main line, just beyond the throat of the railroad's castle-like Windsor Station in Montreal, we waited in the hazy sun of a warm mid-morning for something to happen. It was May 30, 1958— Memorial Day in the United States but a regular Friday in Canada, an important detail. We'd come in search of steam, which now thrived particularly in suburban service, largely a weekday phenomenon.

Just hours earlier we'd arrived on the *Montrealer* from New York City. Nominally a Washington–Montreal service (though by this time only a single sleeper ran through from Washington, with the rest of the consist originating in New York), this work-horse train operated under the joint aegis of the Pennsylvania Railroad, New York, New Haven & Hartford, Boston & Maine, Central Vermont, and Canadian National. Ensconced in Bedroom C of Car 1690, a Pennsy six-bedroom buffet-lounge, we'd left New York's Pennsylvania Station through the East River Tunnels, then climbed the long approach to Hell Gate Bridge, where the East River emptied into Long Island Sound. The Chrysler Building and the Empire State poked their unmistakable silhouettes against the fading pink blush of the western

sky, and pinpricks of office lights speckled the entire skyline.

The overnight rail journey performed its routine magic. When we'd gone to bed we'd been heading north for Hartford, on the NYNH&H, through a landscape alternately urban and suburban. When we awakened in the morning we were in another world, sylvan and northerly: Vermont. Now on CV rails, as we had been since reaching Windsor, we felt we'd as good as arrived in Canada, since we were on a Canadian National subsidiary—and one powered until recently by steam locomotives cut from CNR cloth.

Not long after six, we were at our Pullman's open Dutch door as the *Montrealer* rolled into the St. Albans station, an icon of New England railroading. Leaving nothing to chance, we'd asked the porter to wake us before we arrived. Vinnie Alvino, a traveling companion whose roomette was in the adjacent Pullman, joined us in the vestibule.

The St. Albans station—completed in 1867 and wonderfully archaic, evocative of railroading's earliest days—was a handsome building in two parts, both brick: the three-story, mansard-roofed station itself, which also contained the CV general offices, and the soaring four-track, arched-portaled train shed (razed in 1963).

Leaving St. Albans, we caught our first glimpse of steam—on

At St. Albans, CN Pacific No. 5295 waits to depart for Montreal with the *Ambassador*, having taken over from a Central Vermont RS3.

All photos: Jim Shaughnessy

the dead line west of the tracks, which included a Grand Trunk Mikado and such CV locomotives as an 0-8-0, a 2-8-0, and No. 707, last of the road's impressive 2-10-4's. As we rolled north, Canadian customs and immigration personnel (who had joined the train at St. Albans) walked through the coaches and sleepers, checking credentials and examining suitcases. Though this inspection was routine, an everyday ritual, the border crossing of the *Montrealer* (or, actually, of its southbound counterpart, the *Washingtonian*) was an integral part of the train's lore. In fact, the *Washingtonian* was once known locally as "The Bootlegger," a Prohibition-era moniker alluding to the train's usefulness in smuggling liquor south into the thirsty States.

Before long we were inching across the northern tip of Lake Champlain on the East Alburg trestle, then scooting across the border into Canada. At 8:35 A.M. the *Montrealer* sighed to a stop in the bowels of Canadian National's Central Station, a modern, underground facility without much charm. Virtually across the street, however, was a station of quite another stripe: Canadian Pacific's Windsor, where we headed after hastily dropping our bags at the Laurentian Hotel. This wonderful stone fortress, built in Romanesque style and home to CPR's general offices, was expressive of the dignity and power of Canada's first transcontinental railway and one of the country's great institutions. Opened in February 1889—four years after the last spike was driven at Craigellachie, British Columbia, making CPR a transcontinental enterprise—the headquarters building was designed by Bruce Price and built of native Montreal limestone. Hung proudly on a corner of the building by the time we first saw it was a sign carrying a neon rendering of CPR's wonderful beaver crest, which we'd see on timetables, locomotive cabs, and coaches. "Gare Windsor Station," the sign read.

Montreal Transportation Commission trolleys pass Windsor Station.

The *Canadian* under Windsor Station's trainshed.

Karl Zimmermann

We climbed the stairs to the offices of CPR's Atlantic Region to get a validation stamp on the releases (signed by our parents, a requirement since we were minors) that gave us permission to enter railroad property. (Our parents and their "heirs, executors, administrators and assigns" did "covenant and agree to indemnify and hold harmless the said Canadian Pacific Railway Company, its officers and employees from and against all actions, costs, claims and demands whatsoever," and so forth.)

Now credentialed, we walked through the station's high-ceilinged waiting room. A long row of wrought-iron gates, each capped by a track number and sporting a train destination board, confronted us. All were locked, and the eleven tracks under the Bush train shed (added to the station in 1913) empty of steam—not the sight we'd hoped to see. Blocked by the gates, we walked out into the street and headed west, beyond the fan of station tracks. A few minutes later we scrambled up the embankment to the triple-tracked main leading to the station, then waited to see what might happen along. Plenty did, though mostly the internal-combustion machines on which we lavished little affection.

First, a headlight blinked on under Windsor Station's trainshed, and a pair of Canadian Pacific's colorful F-units (built by General Motors Diesel, a Canadian subsidiary of GM) emerged with a head-end-heavy CPR-CNR "pool train," the *Frontenac*, bound for Quebec City. Its thirteen-car consist, an interesting one that mixed CPR's wine-red stock with CNR cars decked out in green and black, led off with four baggage cars and ended, surprisingly, with a Budd Rail Diesel Car in tow. As the outbound *Frontenac* was passing, an inbound train swung into view: the *Red Wing* from Boston, a joint CPR-Boston & Maine service hauled by one of CPR's rare E8's. (The railroad owned but three of these 2250-horsepower units, which were built in the United States by the Electro-Motive Division of General Motors.) The *Red Wing* rolled by us just as the last few cars of the pool train cleared.

Then we heard another cry of diesel horns, down the tracks where the pool train had headed—toward Westmount, a station just two miles away. From that direction a headlight appeared. It flared and grew, then resolved itself into more diesels, a pair of GMD FP7's leading the *Dominion* through the last few hundred yards of its 2881-mile journey from Vancouver. It sported a

Train 180 from Ste. Thérèse near Montreal West.

Robert F. Collins

mixed consist, including heavyweights and one of the distinctive smooth-sided coaches built by CPR at its Angus Shops. Predominating, however, were fluted stainless-steel cars delivered about four years earlier by The Budd Company for CPR's all-new Montreal/Toronto-to-Vancouver streamliner, the *Canadian*, as well as an upgraded version of the formerly heavyweight *Dominion*, also on that route. A Park-series dome-observation car brought up the rear as the *Dominion* slipped under a signal bridge and jogged through the station leads, coming to a stop at Windsor Station just a few minutes late, not bad after a three-and-a-half-day journey.

Then, finally, we saw what we had come for, as a puff of smoke erupted from under Windsor Station's trainshed. Out backed what had been Train No. 232 from Ottawa: a string of maroon Angus-built coaches, shoved by Royal Hudson No. 2822. This elegant, unique locomotive—which must have sneaked in while we were walking from the station to our trackside vantage point—was the perfect introduction to Canadian steam in the flesh.

The Hudson gleamed, with gray boiler jacket and maroon cab, running-board skirting, and tender panels. Its smooth, moon-faced smokebox, with recessed headlight dead center, was shiny black. At the front end of the running boards were bejeweled crowns in relief. The right to carry these emblems, and the designation "Royal," were bestowed on these streamlined Hudsons in recognition of No. 2850's stint powering the Royal Train, with King George VI and Queen Elizabeth aboard, across Eastern Canada in 1939.

With their 75-inch drivers and sleek good looks, these Royal Hudsons—which numbered 45 all told, built in 1937, 1938, and 1940 by Montreal Locomotive Works—were regal indeed.

As 2822 backed toward Westmount, we followed on foot, as enthralled as the Pied Piper's children.

Logistically as well as aesthetically, Montreal in May of 1958 was an ideal place for novice, pedestrian, locomotive-infatuated young men. Steam of multiple classes was active on both the Canadian Pacific and Canadian National. Windsor Station and Central Station were within shouting distance of each other. The Glen, CPR's engine terminal for Windsor Station, was just adjacent to the Westmount depot and thus easily accessible. The CPR main between Windsor and Westmount was up on a well-treed escarpment, providing acceptable photo locations close at hand. And just below The Glen, off the shoulder of the ridge, was Turcot, CNR's sprawling engine terminal, with a full circle of roundhouse. Look down from The Glen and see Turcot; look up from Turcot and see The Glen. Both vistas were smoky.

In spite of its sylvan-sounding name, The Glen in 1958 was big-time and bustling, servicing a rich mixture of steam and diesel power. Among the latter (which we studiously ignored, shunning all diesels with the ignorant disdain once directed at lepers) were CPR FP7's and FP9's, RS10's, and the rare E8's, Delaware & Hudson RS3's off the daylight *Laurentian* and overnight *Montreal Limited* from New York City, and New York Central's lightning-striped RS3's, power for a single round trip that plied 66 miles south to Malone, New York, in commuter service on Mondays through Fridays. Steam included the Royal Hudsons, semistreamlined G3 Pacifics (akin to but less elegant than the Hudsons), 1200-class light G5 Pacifics, an N2 Consolidation that switched Windsor Station and the coach yards at The Glen, and—rarest of all—one of CPR's unusual 4-4-4 Jubilees, a member of the F1a class, which looked exactly like a telescoped Royal Hudson. Designed for light duty on secondary lines, they had 75-inch drivers (as did the Hudsons) and were hand-fired.

In late morning, when we first saw The Glen, all the locomotives from the inbound commuter rush—still primarily manned by steam, along with some of the new Dayliner RDC's—had arrived, and the hostlers had already bedded down most of them for their siestas in the roundhouse. Fires had been cleaned and tenders refilled from the three-track concrete coaling tower and waterspouts before the engines were set aside to slumber away the midday. We peered into the round-house through windows dusty with soot (though we had permits, we weren't yet bold enough to enter) and watched steam being shined to a high luster—and an F-unit and an E8 too, side by side, looking as though they had just emerged from the paint shop.

The *Frontenac* leaves Windsor Station.   Karl Zimmermann

As befitted these aging steam locomotives, in the twilight of their careers and playing out the string almost exclusively in sub-urban service, the Hudsons and Pacifics and lone Jubilee led mostly undemanding lives, standing idle for much of the day. Three handled commuter trains to Vaudreuil, also called Dorion, 24 miles from Windsor Station, which is where the M&O Subdivision to Ottawa left the Winchester Subdivision to Smiths Falls on the route to Toronto. The run to Vaudreuil took about an hour. Two locomotives went further, to Rigaud, on the Ottawa line, 40 miles from Windsor Station. (This line to Vaudreuil and Rigaud was known as the "Lakeshore" route, serving towns on Lac St. Louis and Lac des Deux Montangnes, wide spots in the St. Lawrence and Ottawa Rivers.) The longest commuter run, at

Royal Hudson 2822 backs Train 232 to The Glen for servicing.   Roger Cook

No. 3642 switches The Glen.   *Roger Cook*

G3 Pacific backs to Windsor Station.   *Karl Zimmermann*

The Glen switcher hauls a consist from Windsor Station.   *Karl Zimmermann*

69 miles, was the lone train to Sutton, on the line to Newport and Wells River, Vermont, which branched off the main line to Saint John, New Brunswick, and the Maritimes at Brookport, just east of Farnham. At this time it was held down by Jubilee 2929. One train ran to Ste. Thérèse, just 26 miles out on an alternate, more northerly line to Ottawa. None of these duties could be considered onerous for locomotives that once sprinted cross-country hauling high-speed limiteds. The most glamorous surviving assignment was on through trains to Ottawa, 111 miles away.

That afternoon we hung out on the plank platform of the Westmount station—a substantial brick structure, appropriately grand for patrons of that upscale suburb. It had a low, gabled center section flanked by square, two-story wings with hipped roofs. The platform was the best place, we figured, to keep tabs on all the action, and we didn't want to miss a thing. The Glen was just opposite, so we could look right across the main-line tracks into the engine terminal and see power being readied for the

Departing Montreal West, Vaudreuil-bound.   *Roger Cook*

road. We could watch yard goat No. 3642 as if it were on stage, and we had orchestra seats. This Consolidation, with black boiler wiped to a shiny luster that gleamed in the afternoon sun, puttered around the yard, switching coaches, baggage cars, and express reefers (which may have come off the *Atlantic Limited* from Saint John, we surmised, laden with fresh fish). Before long, Pacifics, Hudsons, and a Jubilee emerged from the roundhouse and received ritualistic attention—cleaning fires, adding coal, water, and sand, oiling around—before being spotted on the increasingly smoky ready tracks. Then the 3642 began backing glossy maroon passenger consists down the two miles of triple track to Windsor Station, and soon the light engines followed.

The first departure was the 4:10 P.M. for Rigaud—coaches, a combine (perhaps to accommodate the afternoon papers), with G5b Pacific No. 1229 in charge. These 1200's were good-looking, slim-boilered machines whose traditional lines belied their birth dates: 1944 through 1948. A pair of prototypes, 1200 and 1201 (which garnered much fame at and after the end of regular-service steam), were built by CPR at its Angus Shops (with 1201, in fact, being the last locomotive ever built there). They were followed by an even hundred production locomotives from Montreal Locomotive Works. Though postwar locomotives with modern features, they were much akin in appearance to the light-Pacific sisters built some thirty years earlier that they were meant to replace. The G5's were designed by Henry B. Bowen, CPR's chief of motive power from 1928 to 1949; he was a great believer in steam, which no doubt explains the perhaps anomalous construction of more than one hundred light Pacifics at a time when many railroads were thinking diesels.

After 1229 stomped off toward Rigaud, we walked down

The Sutton train climbs the grade from Windsor Station to Westmount (both). *Both photos: Karl Zimmermann*

All photos: Karl Zimmermann

In September 1959, diesels speed Train 232 from Ottawa past Pacific No. 2459 at Rigaud (top left). The following day, Royal Hudson 2822 takes water before departing on a mid-morning local (left), then slows for the flag stop at Dragon (above), where two Montreal-bound ladies shield their heads from the cinders.

toward the brick tower, located right at the east end of the station platform, overlooking the throat where the tracks from the coach yard and engine terminal swung in to join the main line to Windsor Station. Looking up at the windows, we saw the operator waving to us, then beckoning us to come up. We had traded our orchestra seats, somewhat distant, for front-row balcony.

The view, gilded by the warm sun of late afternoon, was spectacular, stretching off into the smoky distance. We could look right into the engine terminal. Just below us, steam shuttled back and forth like trolley cars—light engines dropping down to get their trains, the yard engine batting back and forth, and the commuter rush itself, bearing city workers to their homes in the suburbs. These westbound trains steamed in, shaking the tower's floorboards as they braked for their Westmount stops.

As the trains passed for our review, CPR's spit-and-polish maintenance was manifestly apparent: on the Royal Hudsons, Jubilee, and most G3 semistreamlined Pacifics, shiny gray boiler jackets and glossy maroon side skirting, tender panels, and cabs. (Some of the G3's were all black, and these too shone with a mirror-like luster.) The red coaches were equally sparkling. Most were smooth-sided, lightweight, high-capacity (103-passengers) suburban coaches from among a fleet of forty designed by CPR and built in 1953 by Canadian Car & Foundry Company. Supplementing these were twenty or so circa 1920's heavyweights released from long-distance services as those had begun to dwindle. For that matter the tower itself was neat as a pin, with a bank of gleaming brass pistol grips used to control switches and signals there at the Westmount interlocking.

The highlight of the parade for us was No. 2929, the regular engine at that time on the 4:45 P.M. train to Sutton. This 4-4-4, one of the unique Jubilees, was the last of twenty class F1a

Montreal commuters race to work behind G3 No. 2470.   *Roger Cook*

engines delivered in 1937 and 1938. They weren't quite as distinctive as the five F2a's, Nos. 3000–3004, Montreal Locomotive Works products delivered in 1936—in the fiftieth year of transcontinental service, hence the name "Jubilee." These 3000's had massive pilots, remarkably tall 80-inch drivers (as opposed to the 2900-class's 75-inch), and main rods coupled to the forward drivers (the 2900's were coupled to the rear drivers); designed by H. B. Bowen, they were children of the Depression, designed to haul short, lightweight limiteds on fast schedules with limited stops. The return of business when the Depression eased swelled consists on the premier trains and bumped the Jubilees to local, multi-stop schedules—between Montreal and Quebec, for instance. The less outlandish, smaller-drivered

The Glen.

Karl Zimmermann

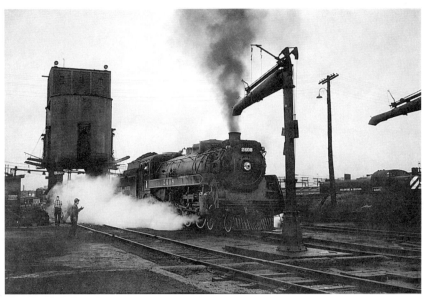

Servicing locomotives at The Glen (all).   *Roger Cook (above and below)*   *Karl Zimmermann*

2900's proved the more useful of the two classes. And 2929 looked plenty exotic to us.

With the Sutton train gone, most of the remaining runs were bound for the Lakeshore route (plus the one to Ste. Thérèse). Lakeshore service on CPR dates back to 1887, when the line was opened to Vaudreuil and CPR went into competition with already established Grand Trunk Railway for what then was regarded as a lucrative passenger trade. (Seventy years later CPR and GTR successor CNR would be all too anxious to turn their backs on it.) In 1890 another railroad, the Montreal & Ottawa, opened a line between Vaudreuil and Rigaud and began mixed train service over it, making connection with the GTR at Vaudreuil. The next year the CPR acquired control of the M&O and, severing connection with the GTR, linked up to its own route, thereby establishing the CPR Lakeshore commuter route

Transfer run for Montreal's St. Luc leaves Hochelaga Yard.   *Roger Cook*

0-8-0-built by American Locomotive Company in Schenectady, New York, and one of four CV switchers that had been transferred to CNR in December 1942 and renumbered. Locomotives from CNR's United States subsidiaries—Central Vermont, Grand Trunk, Grand Trunk Western, and Duluth, Winnipeg & Pacific—periodically were swapped among companies on both sides of the border to meet operational needs.

The next morning we turned our attention to the surviving fragment of Canadian National's Lakeshore commuter operations. It wasn't much, but it was special, thanks to the wonderfully idio-syncratic 4-6-4T Suburbans that powered the trains. At Central Station, just across Dominion Square from Windsor Station and the Laurentian Hotel, we scanned the departure board for the local trains to Dorval. Now hunkering under the Queen

Elizabeth Hotel, at that time part of the Canadian National Hotels chain, 17-track Central Station was opened in 1943. Located at the downtown end of Mount Royal Tunnel, it replaced the 1918 Tunnel Station of Canadian Northern. When Central Station opened, most traffic transferred there from the Grand Trunk Railway's Bonaventure Station as well.

Electrification, which had reached through Mount Royal to Tunnel Station, was extended to steam-electric transfer points at Bridge Street, on the line to the Maritimes that crossed the St. Lawrence on Victoria Bridge, and Turcot, on the line west to Toronto.

In Central Station's cavernous waiting room, we found the proper staircase to descend, then headed for the south, open-air end of the high-level platforms, where we found two remarkable survivors steaming away: Suburban tank engines Nos. 47 and 49. With four wooden coaches, No. 49 would be the first out, while No. 47 would follow with a train of heavyweight cars.

In 1914, a fleet of six of these 4-6-4T's, class X10a, built by Montreal Locomotive Works, entered service on Grand Trunk's "West Island" commuter line to Dorval and Vaudreuil, a route that dates back to well before the turn of the century. These trains originally served Bonaventure Station, remaining there even after Central's opening—until 1948, when Bonaventure suffered a major fire. In 1955, service was cut back from Vaudreuil to Dorval—no great hardship for patrons, since CPR's Lakeshore line directly paralleled CNR's for this stretch, offering plenty of alternative service.

The 4-6-4T's were by design completely bidirectional, since Vaudreuil (their terminus for 41 years) and Dorval had no turning facilities. The small tank and coal bunker held plenty of fuel and water for the short shuttle and allowed the engineer reasonably

Robert F. Collins

Train 287, which will not stop at Dorval, is the second of three evening Lakeshore commuter runs that departed Windsor Station at four-minute intervals between 5:15 and 5:23. There were, in all, five Lakeshore trains. The earliest two, 249 to Rigaud and 287 to Vaudreuil, ran non-stop for some ten miles before making alternating stops beyond Valois. The third train, 289 for Vaudreuil, made all stops, as did the final two departures: 291 for Vaudreuil and 251 for Rigaud.

Eyeball-to-eyeball with No. 47 on the return trip to Montreal.
Karl Zimmermann

Swapping steam power for electric at Turcot.   *Roger Cook*

Northern, the National Transcontinental, and eventually the Grand Trunk Railway and subsidiary Grand Trunk Pacific—in stages, this vast and sometimes redundant coast-to-coast network of lines all became part of the amalgamation.

This is not to say that Canadian National wasn't in many ways a first-class railroad, with some fine steam locomotives. Still, it did seem the blue-collar side of the competition—gritty, scrambling, less glamorous. At Dorval, with its Insulbrick CNR station and its work-stained, oddball 4-6-4T's, the contrast was striking when CPR's Royal Hudsons rolled through.

When No. 49 clanked to a stop at Dorval, we hopped off and made it to the platform just in time to catch Northern No. 6233 roaring through eastbound with a head-end-heavy consist. But it was what happened next that gave the Suburbans and their Dorval turns a measure of notoriety. What happened, like clockwork and as routine as can be, was a "flying switch"—a makeshift expedient associated with countrified, branch-line way freights, hardly what you'd look for in suburban passenger service on one of the nation's two great transcontinental railways.

No. 49 backed its train through the crossover from the westbound main to the eastbound. Then, well east of the switch, the Suburban got up a good head of steam and came chugging toward us. A trainman "pulled the pin," uncoupling the coaches, while the engineer hauled back on the throttle, causing the now-light engine to scoot ahead into the clear on the westbound main. The conductor closed the switch ahead of the free-rolling coaches, which rumbled harmlessly by. As the trainman tied down the coaches' handbrakes, the consist squealed grudgingly to a halt. The 4-6-4T backed through the crossover, then ran ahead to nose up against its train—on the eastbound main, ready to return to Montreal with No. 49's tank leading. As the train waited to

Northern 6233 at Dorval.   *Both photos: Karl Zimmermann*

Branch-line local slows for a power change at Turcot.

Turcot roundhouse (both). *Both photos: Roger Cook*

board passengers, a 2-8-2 came shuffling through with a freight on the now-clear westbound main. No. 49 headed for Montreal, giving way to No. 47, which arrived with a string of heavyweight coaches and performed its flying switch. Meanwhile, G3's shuttled in and out with local trains on the adjacent CPR, and a Royal Hudson stormed through at speed with an express from Ottawa, leaving an impressive pall of smoke in its wake. What a place.

We returned to Montreal on the CNR, riding in the first coach and watching No. 47's smokebox dance in the open forward door. The train stopped at Turcot to swap tank engine for electric motor—No. 182, one of nine box cabs acquired secondhand from the National Harbour Board of Montreal. They'd been built in 1924 by the Dick Kerr Works of the English Electric Company. (The trains could leave Central Station under steam but not arrive, since the locomotive would have to go underground to do that.)

Intrigued by the trolleys we'd seen from the train, at Turcot we hopped one of the cars, veterans built in 1930, and rode out to Lachine and back, on the 91 Line along the Lachine Canal. Then we disembarked and entered the steamy world of Turcot.

Compared to the bustle of The Glen, in fact, Turcot's steam activity was modest and diffused by the time of our visits. It was in any event far less predictable and concentrated than the CPR commuter show. Still, Turcot was special—the largest and busiest roundhouse on the CNR. The facility was opened by the Grand Trunk shortly after the turn of the century and grew in stages to become a completely circular structure with 56 stalls. In the St. Henri district of the city, the yard and shops were located on what had been Turcot Swamp, and the facilities perched on landfill.

Up on the hill at The Glen, in the land of shiny gray and red and semistreamling, modern passenger steam was six-coupled, Pacifics and Hudsons. CPR's only eight-coupled passenger power was a pair of Northerns built in 1928. We never saw them. On the other hand, down below, in CNR land, Northerns were the culminating design, and basic black the look. Though CNR did build a few Hudsons, five in all, elegantly high-drivered and colorful in green accents, we'd have to wait for a trip to Toronto the following spring to meet them.

In Montreal, at Turcot, Northerns ruled, a design evolution that began on CNR in 1927 and continued right up through 1944, when the last (and, lacking the beetle-browed look of the

Maritimes-bound tonnage east of St. Lambert.

Jim Shaughnessy

35

Ex-Central Vermont 0-8-0 switches MDT reefers at Turcot.　　*Roger Cook*

An 0-8-0 on the Turcot roundhouse lead.　　*Karl Zimmermann*

smokebox-mounted Elesco feedwater heater, perhaps least aesthetic) of the CNR 4-8-4's were built. (The first 4-8-4, No. 6100, carried the designation "Confederation" on its running board, since its delivery fell on the sixtieth anniversary of Canadian Confederation. The Northern Pacific-derived term "Northern" soon became the norm, however.)

We circled the roundhouse, carefully inspecting each locomotive. Most of the newer power—Northerns, Mountains, and one 2-10-2—had that distinctive Canadian National front-end look: Elesco feedwater heater, vee number boards, centered headlight, boiler-tube pilot, and cast brass number plate with raised numerals between the words "Canadian" above and "National" below, all against a bright red background. (This number-plate style had originated with predecessor Canadian Northern.) The Northerns also carried cast-brass cylinder plates that read "Northern Type."

The older Suburbans, Pacifics, Mikados, Ten-Wheelers, Consolidations, and switchers also had the CNR genes—though, except for the Suburbans, Mikes, and some Pacifics, they lacked the imposing Elescos that made CNR steam locomotives look larger than their statistics showed. Most of the engines we encountered on our circuit of the roundhouse were cold—stored or awaiting the scrap line.

We especially noted No. 4190 as the sole 2-10-2 on hand. It was one of the five Class T2a's that, when delivered in 1924, had been the largest locomotives in the British Empire. Designed with 57-inch drivers for slow-speed, heavy transfer service in the Toronto area, this one example of the class subsequently had been transferred to Montreal for similar duty. They were further notable as the first Canadian engines with Vanderbilt tenders. We also singled out Northern 6258—among the final Northerns built, in the series without Elescos, but with a one-of-a-kind

Dorval-bound Suburbans at sunrise at Central Station (both).

number plate: round, with a raised maple-leaf design.

On the ready track, we found Northern No. 6212 with its engineer oiling around. A brand-new driver (its lack of white striping stood out like a sore thumb) bore testimony to a recent visit to the backshop. This was a locomotive whose number we recognized.

Morgan and Hastings had encountered the 6212 in 1955 on a freight at Cantic, Quebec—newly shopped, with freshly laundered white flags mounted on its glossy black boiler. In the last installment of *Trains* Magazine's "Steam in Indian Summer" series, Morgan characterized this Northern as "an engine with a future," which it clearly was, though perhaps not as long a future as we or Morgan would have liked. But then again, no steam engines did have, even in Canada.

Both photos: Roger Cook

No. 6034 with Train 28 from Stratford.

Roger Cook

LAST CITADEL OF CANADIAN NATIONAL STEAM

For steam fans, reliable information was hard to come by in the late 1950's, so whenever an issue of *Trains* Magazine showed up in our mailboxes we avidly scanned every page for news—reassignments, new discoveries, or, more often than not, retirements. By August 1958 we'd already made one trip to Montreal and had our Pullman reservations for a return visit, so when that month's *Trains* arrived, we turned eagerly to an 11-page photo essay by Don Wood and John Rehor titled "Dominion Doings in Steam."

That article put a new idea in our heads: that perhaps an entirely different Canadian steam world existed west of Montreal—in Ontario. Wood's and Rehor's wonderful black-and-whites showed steam power of various ages and wheel arrangements: a turn-of-the-century CNR 2-6-0 and 4-6-0's belonging to both CNR and CPR working branch lines, a CPR 3000-class 4-4-4, a cone-nosed CNR 4-8-2, two CNR 4-8-4's meeting with passenger trains in tow. Although we'd return to Montreal within weeks, we now had Ontario on our minds.

So the following winter, when we learned that CNR was consolidating all its remaining Eastern steam in southern Ontario and at Toronto in particular, we were ready to go. Thus it happened

Mountain and Northern at Spadina.   *Jim Shaughnessy*

No. 6402 backing from Spadina to Union Station.

Karl Zimmermann

that, on April Fool's Day in 1959, we raised the shade of Bedroom F in our Toronto-bound Pullman to see the wine country of the Niagara Peninsula in the first blush of dawn. Our New York Central 11-bedroom sleeper had left Grand Central Terminal at 7:15 the evening before as part of the Central's *Detroiter*. At about 5 A.M. in Buffalo, we'd been shuffled into the consist of Toronto, Hamilton & Buffalo's Train 371 and acquired for power the pair of maroon-and-cream TH&B hood units that we could see on the head end when we craned our necks to look out the window.

Plenty excited, we dressed early and headed for the diner-lounge for breakfast. We were tucking into our bacon and eggs when, after departing TH&B's Art Deco Hunter Street Station in Hamilton and now on CPR rails, our train snaked through the switches at Hamilton Junction. Hamilton was a gritty steel city and, on our right, we saw clouds of gray smoke belching from the Steel Company of Canada and Dominion Foundries & Steel blast furnaces, which lined the harbor. Then, to the left, we caught our first glimpse of steam: a well-worn CNR 2-8-2 on the side track at Bayview Junction, waiting to help the next westbound freight to Copetown.

Bayview Junction was the east leg of a wye whose other points were Hamilton Junction and Hamilton West. At Bayview, CNR's Toronto–Sarnia main line diverged upgrade (as the Dundas Subdivision) toward Dundas, Copetown, and points west, while the CNR line to Niagara Falls and Buffalo curved along the harbor toward Hamilton. Most passenger trains on the Toronto–Sarnia line served Hamilton directly—by back-up moves via Bayview Junction into or out of CNR's James Street Station—and those that bypassed the city made bus connections at Dundas, six miles away. Parallel to CNR's tracks between Hamilton Junction and Hamilton West, and on a steeper grade,

was CPR's Goderich Subdivision, climbing to Guelph Junction on its meandering way to Lake Huron.

From Bayview, aboard our sleeper from New York, we sped toward Toronto on CNR's double-track Oakville Subdivision, also used by CPR trains between Hamilton Junction and Toronto. (We were one of those, since No. 371 had been taken over by CPR at Hamilton, now running eastbound as Canadian Pacific No. 322. All trains from Buffalo and Niagara Falls changed their numbers at Hamilton to reflect change of direction.) The combination of CNR and CPR traffic made the Oakville Sub the busiest mainline in Canada. (Had we been traveling a few years earlier, we might have been riding behind steam east of Hamilton, since Buffalo–Toronto passenger trains swapped TH&B diesels for CPR steam at Hamilton. Now the diesels ran right through to Toronto.)

As our train neared Toronto, we staked out both sides of our sleeper, searching for signs of active steam. At Mimico, Canadian National's main Toronto-area freight yard and the engine terminal for freight power, telltale white smoke tantalized us, but boxcars blocked our view. A few miles later, approaching Toronto Union Station for an on-time 8:45 A.M. arrival, we spotted CNR's Spadina Avenue roundhouse, its smoky ready tracks populated by various passenger power: 5700-series Hudsons and 6200- and 6400-series Northerns. We hardly noticed CPR's John Street roundhouse, just beyond the CNR facility, for its air was smokeless. But with the steamy scene at Spadina, we knew we had arrived.

We hurried off the train. Though we were staying right across the street at the Royal York—Canadian Pacific's magnificent hotel, the largest in the British Empire when opened in 1929— we doubted that our room would be ready and so checked our

Hamilton commuter run ready to leave Union Station.

"Pool train" for Belleville.

bags at the station. Opened in 1927 and a direct precursor to the Royal York, Toronto Union Station is a masterpiece. Its vaulted, columned great hall is encircled with a frieze listing far-flung destinations served by CPR and CNR, who shared the station. To all this we gave short shrift, however. With the signed releases (which we'd received by mail) in our pockets, we hoofed it back down the tracks toward Spadina Avenue. Only after we got there did we realize that, in our haste, we'd forgotten to pick up timetables at the station's imposing bank of ticket windows. What might be coming, we wondered?

Youthful exuberance was soon rewarded (and forgetfulness forgiven) by the sight of CNR Mountain No. 6034 with what we later surmised was Train 28 from Stratford. Here was what we'd come for: heavy CNR power hauling mainline passenger trains. We got our shots, then hurried on to the roundhouse, where 4-8-4's 6214 and 6402 were being serviced. The 6402 was one of five 77-inch-drivered streamlined Northerns that had once handled premier passenger trains between Montreal and Sarnia and were now running their final miles, primarily in Hamilton–Toronto commuter service. Sister 6404 was also there; we learned that it had arrived from Niagara Falls the previous evening.

Built in 1936 by Montreal Locomotive Works, Northerns 6400-6404 were Canada's first streamlined steam, getting in ahead of CPR's Royal Hudsons and Jubilees. And the Northerns were the more thoroughly streamlined—shrouded, with shovel-nose front and boiler-top cowling. This casing had a practical purpose: smoke-deflection. Through the 1930's CNR and Canada's National Research Council had studied the problem of engineers' visibility being limited by smoke. Wind-tunnel tests suggested that protruding stacks and domes were the culprit in causing smoke to swirl low, so CNR's five Northerns—plus the

No. 6402 departs with Train 79 for Hamilton. An hour later, 6230 will follow with Train 81.

All photos: Roger Cook

six near-identical sisters built in 1938 by Lima Locomotive Company for CNR Stateside subsidiary Grand Trunk Western— were fully streamlined. When put to the test of regular service, the cowling seemed of dubious benefit, and many enginemen took a dim view of the 6400's, feeling that the streamlining actually directed the smoke right in their faces.

Though it gained less fame than CPR's Hudson 2850 for doing so, No. 6400 also powered the Royal Train in 1939, tricked out in Royal Blue for the assignment. It then went on to the New York World's Fair, joined by the Royal Hudson in representing the newest and most stylish in Canadian railroading.

Pacific 5267 was under the six-silo concrete coal dock, and Hudsons 5702 and 5703 steamed on an adjacent track. (We ignored the Montreal Locomotive Works FPA4's, GMD FP9's, and Canadian Locomotive Company C-Liners idling on the ready tracks.) Though the Hudsons were not fully streamlined like the 6400's, even at rest their uniquely tall, white-tired drivers implied motion. When CNR placed them in service in the late 1930's, the company touted them as the fastest locomotives in Canada. Though slightly less powerful than CPR's Hudsons, their 80-inch drivers (versus 75-inch on CPR's engines) gave them an edge in top speed, though not in versatility.

The CNR Hudsons had clean-lined, distinctive good looks, with front-mounted brass bells flanked by angled number boards, fluted stacks, and olive-green paint applied to their wide-paneled running boards, cabs, and rounded Vanderbilt tenders. They were unlike any other locomotives we'd ever encountered. All these CNR steam locomotives except the 6200-class, non-streamlined Northerns were new to us. Whether in liveries of standard black or olive green, they became instant favorites. What were missing, though, were the distinctive cone-nosed Mountains, or "Bullet-

Just in from London, No. 5701 is at Spadina.   *Both photos: Karl Zimmermann*

Nosed Bettys." "Gone West," the roundhouse foreman told us, for conversion to oil and service on the Manitoba prairies.

Also missing was CPR's spit and polish. We'd gotten our ideas about Canadian locomotive maintenance from seeing the CPR Pacifics and Hudsons lovingly buffed up by the shop forces at The Glen. On the other hand, CNR's Montreal engines had been sooty and grimy—though aside from the 4-6-4T's (no models of maintenance themselves) this power was largely in freight service. CNR's Spadina passenger power also tended toward the unkempt; some engines were cleaner than others, but none could hold a candle to the CPR power we remembered from The Glen. That the Hudsons and streamlined Northerns were tricked out in green, however, gave them a stylish look.

Train 80 arriving Toronto from London.

Train 28 arrives from Stratford.

Karl Zimmermann

3409 steamed west on the bypass with a mixed freight in tow, it too showed up the 2856.

But steam was making its last stand, and it looked it. While Pacific 5292, brown all over with a thick layer of grit, was being serviced that afternoon for a local to Belleville via the Uxbridge Subdivision to Lindsay, we noticed what appeared to be a leaking side panel on its tender. By the time the Pacific departed at 5:35 P.M. with just a baggage car and single coach, a stream of water was spouting from the tender's left side. All in all, the 5292 was a sorry sight.

We had come to Toronto well prepared; in addition to Spadina, we also had releases for CNR's Mimico and CPR's Lambton roundhouses. Since we hoped to see active freight power at both, the next morning we took off on a circle tour to visit these facilities. We left Union Station at 7 A.M. aboard London-bound Train 77 for a 17-minute trip to Mimico—a stop scheduled to accommodate CNR workers. The roundhouse there was well populated with Northerns, Mountains, Mikados, a few Pacifics, and smaller power. Some engines were under steam, but the ready tracks held only diesels. Crestfallen, we learned that we were a week too late for real action. Some steam still was being dispatched, but its use was sporadic and its destinations— including Fort Erie, Niagara Falls, London, Stratford, and Sarnia—diverse.

By April 1959, passenger steam at CPR's John Street roundhouse had been relegated to occasional stand-by service; during our Toronto sojourn, no locomotive there turned a wheel nor was even steamed. In fact, the only active CPR passenger engine we did see was in freight service. It was Royal Hudson No. 2856, which we spotted plodding westbound on the "High Line," the bypass track just south of Union Station. We were shocked at the dusty patina of soot it carried; suddenly those "dirty" Spadina engines looked a good deal spiffier in comparison. When, not far behind the Royal Hudson, CNR Mikado

At Lambton, the story was similar: Pacifics, Mikados, Ten-Wheelers, and Consolidations filled the stalls, but nothing was happening. It became painfully apparent that, without the range and flexibility of an automobile, we would have to give up on photographing active CPR steam. So we retreated, by bus and subway, to downtown Toronto and Union Station. We were disappointed but not defeated, for we knew that Spadina's steam was active, dependable, and accessible.

Before long our spirits were lifted by streamlined Northern 6402's departure with the first of two commuter runs to Hamilton. Then at 6:15 P.M. Train 37 steamed west for Stratford behind Hudson No. 5703, with the golden light of a late-winter afternoon glowing on every graceful angle of the locomotive. Finally, at dusk, Northern 6226 followed with the second Hamilton train.

Stratford was a name we knew. The Grand Trunk had established locomotive shops there in 1871, and they had grown to become a major CNR facility. Were the shops still active, we wondered, and could any of those cone-nosed Mountains missing from Spadina be there for conversion from coal to oil-firing? What else steamy might be happening there?

Our timetable showed that Train 37 terminated at Stratford, while other passenger trains turned south to London, on the Toronto–Sarnia main. From Stratford, we could have ridden north to Palmerston or sampled mixed trains west on a branch to Sarnia or east all the way to Fort Erie via Brantford and Caledonia. Actually, we could have reached Palmerston directly, via Guelph, and the lines from there were even more intriguing. The train from Toronto continued on to Owen Sound, a port on

Continued on page 65

No. 6403 leaves Grimsby for Niagara Falls.   *Jim Shaughnessy*

Westbound at Burlington on the Oakville Subdivision.

All photos: Jim Shaughnessy

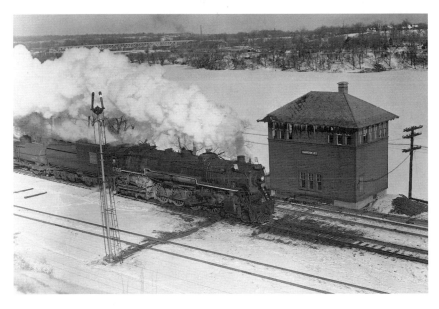

Icicles hang from the eaves on a bitterly cold February afternoon as trains pass the interlocking tower at Hamilton Junction (all).

The *Inter-City Limited* from Chicago storms through Hamilton Junction bound for Toronto.

Both photos: Jim Shaughnessy

A short Canadian Pacific freight makes a run at the hill, which begins here.

Triple meet at Guelph, below. Hamilton–Owen Sound Train 173 had been waiting on the center track when—almost simultaneously, at 9:40 A.M.—Mountain 6014 arrived from Toronto with London-bound Train 29 and Owen Sound–Toronto Train 172 appeared behind a Pacific. Connecting passengers must detour around 6014, which is blocking the crosswalk. On a brighter morning, Pacific 5607 (left) heads for Owen Sound with Train 173, passing the caboose of a Pacific-powered freight that had just arrived from London.

Both photos: Don Wood

At Stratford, Mountain 6007 has arrived from Toronto.

Jim Shaughnessy

Dorothy and the Duck Inn

In 1957 John Rehor and I were looking for a place to stay in Stratford after shooting the steam action between there and St. Mary's. It was getting late and, before going out to take some night shots, we wanted to get our lodging all squared away. We found this little place—today you'd probably say it was a bed and breakfast—called the Duck Inn. Dorothy was the owner, and, when we told her we wanted a couple of nights' lodging, she was very agreeable. Then we went on to say that we needed a room we could darken during the day.

That took her aback. And when we saw that she was uneasy, we naturally decided to string her along a little bit. But eventually we explained that we were photographers and had to change film from holders to film boxes. If we couldn't get the room dark we'd have to have a closet—somewhere we could be sure there'd be no light. Such are the hardships of shooting with a Speed Graphic and using sheet film.

We found a hall closet and equipped it with a little table. First I'd go and do my changing and loading and John would sit

Train 40 at Stratford awaits its scheduled 8:40 P.M. departure for Toronto. *All photos: Don Wood*

outside and make sure nobody opened the door. After that he went in and I sat guard. Even then we knew this stuff was valuable, so everything had to be A-okay. It all worked out, though. We didn't have one fogged negative.

The next year we went back again to the Duck Inn.

"Oh, yeah," Dorothy said, "you're the two guys that like to be in the dark."

"We're in the dark about everything," John answered.

—*Don Wood*

London–Owen Sound Train 168 at and then leaving St. Marys (both).

At Stratford, Pacific 5594 has replaced 5588 on Train 168 to Owen Sound, while 5287 waits with Train 28 for Toronto.

Jim Shaughnessy

Roger Cook

The Wabash Railroad's Midwestern United States lines reached from Detroit eastward across southern Ontario on CNR trackage rights. At Fort Erie, an important interchange yard across the Niagara River from Buffalo, Wabash blue, gray, and silver F-units added a splash of color to the gritty environment populated by CNR locomotives such as Mikados 3431 and 3496.

Jim Shaughnessy

Galt.

Cab Ride to Orr's Lake

Hanging around the station at Guelph Junction on a hot day in August 1957, I got to talking with one of the railroaders—a friendly guy named Frank Bunker, who turned out to be the engineer on a Pacific spotted across from the station. His engine would be the helper on a westbound train of empty passenger cars deadheading to Windsor.

"Do you want to take a ride?" Bunker asked. Normally I would have declined, since I generally wanted to take pictures along the line. But for whatever reason, this time it seemed like a good idea, so I said "sure!"

Before long the passenger special from Toronto pulled in behind a Royal Hudson and stopped at the station, where the helper was added. Now a doubleheader, the train waited for a diesel-powered freight to clear eastbound. After the meet I climbed aboard the helper, and the special moved out of the station— only to be held in the yard for another meet, this one with a steam freight.

After the meet I walked back and boarded the Royal Hudson before we finally headed west. Though it was heavy going on the grade, we flew along pretty good. When we got to Orr's Lake, the helper cut off and ran ahead, then backed into the siding to let the Royal Hudson continue west with its train. I rode back to Guelph Junction on the helper with Frank Bunker. I guess he must have been a closet buff, since I learned years later that he stayed involved with steam and ran on some of the Ontario Rail excursions in the 1970's.

In any case, I'm glad I accepted his invitation to climb up and ride. I enjoyed it immensely.

—Jim Shaughnessy

Headed for Orr's Lake.

Royal Hudson 2857's engineer.

All photos: Jim Shaughnessy

Engineer Frank Bunker climbs aboard the now-light helper at Orr's Lake (top left), where it waits for orders (left) before returning to Guelph Junction. Above, 2236 meets sibling 2235 and a Mikado lugging freight at Guelph Junction.

Canadian Pacific's Jubilee No. 3000 is near the end of its operating life at Glencoe in July 1957. (In fact, three of the class of five had already been retired.) Though designed to haul short trains of lightweight cars at high speeds on the Toronto–Windsor, Montreal–Quebec, and Calgary–Edmonton routes, 3000 has been relegated to Train 634, a head-end-heavy Windsor–London local. With 80-inch drivers and main rod connected to the lead driver, the Jubilee's wheelbase was 37 feet—just two feet shorter than a 75-inch-drivered 2800 Hudson. Unfortunately, specialized design limited the class's usefulness, and all were gone by late 1958.

Both photos: Don Wood

The sun is setting west of the Spadina Avenue overpass, and its last rays illuminate the 80-inch drivers and cylindrical Vanderbilt tender of Canadian National Hudson No. 5702 as its fire is cleaned. Soon after this April 1, 1959, tableau, 5702's fire would be dropped forever.

Both photos: Roger Cook

Mountain 6034 departs for Stratford.

All photos: Karl Zimmermann

Georgian Bay of Lake Huron, and there was direct Hamilton–Owen Sound service via Guelph as well. In fact, passenger and mixed-train service radiated from Palmerston in all directions: not just to Owen Sound but also north on the branch to Durham, northwest to Southampton on Lake Huron, southwest to Listowel (where one line continued south to Stratford and another southwest before tacking northerly to Kincardine, also on Lake Huron), and southwest toward Guelph, junction with the Toronto–Stratford line. From Guelph, yet another line continued south to Preston and Galt and on to Lyndon, where it connected with the Toronto–Sarnia main line.

Our third morning in Toronto, under a slate-gray sky, we moped around Union Station, wondering if we shouldn't have been more adventurous. Perhaps, for instance, we should have ridden out to Stratford the night before instead of playing it safe on now-familiar ground. Except for the two commuter runs from Hamilton, a Pacific on the Uxbridge Sub train from Belleville, and the train from Stratford, we saw only diesels. And it rained. Aside from shots of 6402 storming past 6230 (both on Hamilton commuter runs), the day was a photographic bust. Our mood was as gray as the weather.

On Saturday, our last day in Toronto, we parted the curtains of our room at the Royal York Hotel and were heartened to see an early-morning sky of hazy blue. We posted ourselves just east of the Spadina Avenue Bridge, opposite the roundhouse, to shoot the morning's sole commuter run from Hamilton. About 7:30, billows of white smoke appeared beyond a line of boxcars, and the now-familiar 6402 chuffed toward us, its blunt snout momentarily bathed in steam as it rolled under Spadina Avenue. The baggage car and short string of heavyweight coaches hardly taxed the big streamliner.

With the Royal York in the background, 6213 heads east with a passenger extra.

Spadina ready tracks.

Westbound CNR freight on the "High Line."

Both photos: Karl Zimmermann

Later, after 6402 had been coaled and watered, we realized a Hudson and a Northern were being readied for eastbound runs. By late morning, 5703 was steaming softly under the train shed, ready to depart on the 11:30 "pool train" for Belleville. Soon after it left, 6213 rolled light through the shed, then backed against a string of coaches. Secured on both sides of the feedwater heater were clean white flags indicating that her train was an extra; we never did learn where it was headed.

Now only hours remained before our 8:35 P.M. departure. Again we headed to trackside near Spadina Avenue. A pillar of white smoke confirmed that 6402 was ready to leave Union Station for Hamilton. Then, suddenly, a contrasting cloud of black smoke erupted from under the train shed. What could this be?

No. 2856 works freight westbound past Union Station.

Then we recognized the maroon-and-gray livery of CPR diesels rapidly accelerating a string of maroon heavyweights towards us from under that cloud of what we now realized was diesel exhaust. They were back-to-back MLW RS10's, and we snapped a picture as the shiny, smoking units passed— our first and last diesel shot of the trip.

Moments later, 6402's train departed, heading straight into that low afternoon sun. Steam following diesel, heading into the sunset, we thought as we walked slowly back toward Union Station. We were sad to be leaving, knowing that, when we did, we'd be saying goodbye forever to Toronto steam. At the station,

therefore, reluctant to call it a day until the sun had set, we lingered on the platform. Then, at twilight, the last pink light illuminated a boxy tender backing toward us. It was Mountain No. 6034, the first locomotive we had seen on our first day, now backing into Union Station to pick up Train 37 for Stratford.

Our first train had become our last. And though hardly prizewinners, our slightly fuzzy, underlit photographs of that westbound departure are precious nonetheless, for within weeks steam was all but dead at Spadina. On April 23, No. 6234 left Toronto on Train 79 for Hamilton and returned the next morning

Northern 6402 leaves Toronto for Hamilton.

All photos: Karl Zimmermann

on Train 76. That evening, 79 headed west with a diesel in charge, and steam in regularly scheduled Canadian National passenger service in Ontario was history.

So we counted ourselves lucky to have seen what we did, though youth and inexperience had anchored us at Toronto. We'd seen trains leaving for Stratford, for Hamilton, for London, for Belleville, and had wished we could follow them there, expanding our opportunities and understanding beyond the narrow if busy hub of Spadina Avenue and Toronto Union Station. Other photographers—those older, wiser, more adventurous, and more mobile—did of course venture out on the spokes, exploring the destinations and destinies of the steam trains that we saw begin their journeys under the Toronto trainshed. Jim Shaughnessy, Don Wood, Bob Collins, and others were all out there, recording steam in its final years—creating photographic images that gave honest shape to our imaginings.

No. 5703 on Train 37 for Stratford (both).

Train M559 between Norton and Case.

Robert F. Collins

BRANCH LINE CANADA

*I*n our world of 1950's railroading—an era of precipitously declining steam that remained richer in the appurtenances of traditional railroading than we then had the wit to appreciate— certain lines and locales had almost talismanic significance as archetypes. We thought of Union Pacific's Sherman Hill route, for instance, as the acme of high-density, high-horsepower Western steam railroading, with its Big Boys, Challengers, and Northerns. Nickel Plate's Berkshire-powered fast-freight line typified merchandise expediters. Norfolk & Western's Y6-powered drags through Virginia were the spirit of coal railroading incarnate.

For the image of the quintessential branch line—light power, light traffic, light rail, wooden coaches, mixed trains, rural ways— our thoughts turned north, to an obscure (from owner Canadian Pacific's point of view) line in remote New Brunswick: the 44.6-mile branch that, running north-south, linked Chipman and Norton. This was coal country, somewhere between Saint John and Moncton and nowhere. Running through empty, evergreen landscapes, the branch was indeed a line of light rail and, even more to the point, light bridges. By the mid-fifties, it was home to the oldest, lightest, rarest locomotives running in Canada: a trio of American Standards built in the 1880's.

The oldest of all, No. 136, had been constructed by Rogers Locomotive Works in Paterson, New Jersey, in 1883. Somewhat

Late morning layover in Chipman.   *Robert F. Collins*

akin visually (both, for instance, had 63-inch drivers) was No. 144, an 1886 product of CPR's DeLorimier Shops in Montreal. The youngster of the group—and the most graceful, with 70-inch drivers—was No. 29, built in 1887, also at DeLorimier Shops. All were significantly rebuilt at Angus Shops in 1912, when they acquired their current numbers.

Their survival, of course, had nothing to do with history or sentiment. It had everything to do with weight restrictions on a pair of endearingly flimsy bridges—bridges that wouldn't carry

even the modest heft of CPR's little D4g Ten-Wheelers, which prowled other of CPR's light branches. One span was right at Norton, an iron bridge across the Kennebecasis River. Another, between Washademoak and Cody, was a non-interlocked drawbridge across an arm of Washademoak Lake. (A third, Pennlyn trestle, was replaced by a steel bridge before the end of steam.)

The Chipman-Norton branch had been completed in 1890 as part of the Central Railway Company (New Brunswick), which had the mission of linking Frederickton, the provincial capital, with a new port to be built on the Bay of Fundy. Like so many early railroad projects, this one never worked out as planned.

At Norton, the Central Railway connected with the Intercolonial Railway (later part of CNR); at Chipman (where the line interchanged with the National Transcontinental Railway, also eventually part of CNR), it turned southeast to the coal town of Minto and eventually (after convoluted corporate transformations) on to Fredericton and linkage with the rest of the CPR.

In 1959, with the trio of 4-4-0's on borrowed time, as was the branch itself, the operation occupied little more than a column half-inch in CPR's 25-page section of the *Official Guide*. Table 7 informed us that M559, the daily-except-Sunday mixed, left Norton at 8 A.M. (it was an hour later in summer) and arrived Chipman at 10:50; on the return, as M560, it left at 12:35 P.M. and tied up at Norton at 3:05. What this tiny entry didn't suggest was the romance of diminutive locomotives hauling a wooden, truss-rodded combine and the occasional freight car through such places as Belle Isle, Scotch Settlement, Bagdad, and Young's Cove Road.

John Meyers was the regular engineer on the Chipman–Norton mixed, and CPR historian Omer Lavallée believed him largely responsible for the longevity of the 4-4-0's. Meyers lived in

No. 425 westbound on the Waltham Sub.   *Karl Zimmermann*

Norton; after his locomotive had been parked in the single-stall enginehouse for the night, he would often work on it himself and on his own time.

With his help, the 4-4-0's soldiered on nearly to the end of Canadian steam—until the branch was dieselized in October 1959, when 44-ton diesel-hydraulic No. 18, built by Canadian Locomotive Company, was transferred there from Ontario. The diesel made its first run October 16, and shortly thereafter, with the fall timetable change, the mixed's schedule was adjusted to make Chipman the overnight terminal. There No. 18 shared the enginehouse with the 4-4-0's, which were relegated to standby service. The 144's tubes were about to expire, so it was shipped to Montreal, where it ran on a pair of November excursions before being donated to the Canadian Railroad Historical Association. After that there were brief reprieves for steam when the diesel broke down. No. 136 was used in January 1960 and No. 29 for the entire first week of March.

Morning departure eastbound from Campbell's Bay.
Karl Zimmermann

Coaling up at Chipman.

Robert F. Collins

Employees are advised that "trains must not exceed four miles per hour over Bridge Mileage 90.08," and Train M560 (below) is adhering to the speed restriction as it crawls across the iron span to reach CNR's Norton station on the Kennebecasis River's east bank. The next morning, April 25, 1959, M559 (right) is ready to depart for Chipman at 8 A.M.

Both photos: Robert F. Collins

On the Waltham Subdivision, D4g Ten-Wheeler No. 425 in early morning at Campbell's Bay.

Karl Zimmermann

But we never made it to Chipman and Norton, so far was it from home—and, for that matter, from everything. However, the Waltham Subdivision, an 80-mile branch running northwest from Ottawa into the Pontiac region, was no slouch for charm, either. And we did get there for steam. Barely.

In early September of 1959, taking advantage of a long Labor Day weekend (which we expanded even further) before going back to school, we headed for Ottawa in Vinnie Alvino's Buick. We were, looking back on it, woefully ill informed, but sometimes it's better to be lucky than smart. Vinnie had heard that some steam might be operating out of Ottawa West engine terminal, so we decided to swing by—essentially a detour on a trip to Montreal. We arrived late on a Thursday morning with uncertain expectations but high hopes. Scanning the ready tracks and servicing facilities for locomotives under steam, we found exactly nothing. Though we saw some Ten-Wheelers and Pacifics, everything was cold—stored or in standby service, we learned, but in any case not needed at the moment.

In the roundhouse, however, behind closed doors, there was something: D4g Ten-Wheeler No. 425 with fire in its grates, just beginning to build up steam.

"She's going out this afternoon on the Waltham mixed," the roundhouse foreman told us. "We're getting her hot now. Lately the job's been getting a diesel every day but Thursday. Lucky you're here today."

Waltham? That sent us scrambling for our Esso roadmap of Quebec, which (as was the welcome custom in those days) showed rail lines as well as roads. On the map we traced the branch's light-blue crosshatching as it bridged the Ottawa River into Quebec at Hull, then ran west to Quyon, Shawville, Campbell's Bay, and Fort Coulogne before petering out at Waltham, a modest com-

Ottawa West. *Roger Cook*

munity at best to be the terminus of a branch. CPR men knew this line as the "Pontiac" for the region it traversed, and because the track west of Aylmer was built as the grandly named Pontiac Pacific Junction Railway Company.

No. 425, which we thought a very pretty little engine, was a light 4-6-0 built in 1912 by CPR at its Angus Shops. Its survival in steam until 1959, long after its bigger and newer compatriots had been retired, was due to branch-line weight restrictions—the

Chipman-Norton scenario all over again. (In fact, the Waltham Subdivision for years had been worked by 4-4-0's, and at least two of Chipman-Norton's famous final three had put in time there.)

"Wretched little machines" is the epithet hung on the D4g's by Duncan du Fresne, who fired them on the Waltham Sub and later wrote about them without affection for Bytown Railway Society's *Branchline*. They were, he recalled, "short-coupled, top-heavy, narrow-fireboxed, jouncy," and "literally bounced down the track somewhere between the right-of-way fences."

Such hard-nosed realism would surely have surprised us; we assumed, naturally, that the enginemen who ran these steam machines shared our boyish enthusiasm for them, that for them too diesels were anathema, the dreaded interlopers. No doubt this was not entirely wrong, since many railroaders did regard these dinosaurs with some affection and pride. How else to explain the fact that, after the 425 poked its nose out of the roundhouse and was spun on the turntable, a shop laborer spray-painted the rust-streaked smokebox a shiny black? This was done, most likely, at the behest of the roundhouse foreman, who knew we were going to be photographing the engine. Wind carried the fine spray in our direction, and we ended up hurriedly wiping black speckles from our camera lenses.

No. 425 had the distinction of being the first of the 75 D4g's, built from 1912 to 1915, yet it was not the lowest numbered. When erected, the Ten-Wheelers were assigned blocks of numbers out of chronological sequence; 425 to 492 were delivered first, followed by 417 to 424 (using numbers freed by older 4-6-0's as they were retired). Thus 425 was the first built and 424 the last.

The D4g's were designed specifically for branch-line assignments. Rather than continue upgrading its older, lighter locomotives with new boilers and superheaters, CPR management opted for a "modern" design to join its eminently successful D10 Ten-Wheelers, which had proven their worth in a variety of assignments since 1905. (Five hundred and two D10's were built before construction ceased in 1913, at which time one in every seven CPR locomotives was a D10.) But the D10's were too heavy for many lightly constructed secondary lines, so the D4g was born—for reasons not unlike a later management generation's thinking when it designed the G5 Pacifics to replace in kind its over-30-year-old G1's and G2's.

After coaling up from the angled tin-can coaling tower and topping off its tender at the water plug, 425 backed down to Ottawa Union Station and coupled onto a modest consist: just a lightweight Angus Shops-built mail and express car and a heavyweight coach. Though officially a mixed train, No. M653, it carried no freight cars on this September day, a common enough occurrence in the mixed's final months of operation. (In addition to the daily-except-Sunday mixed, there was a triweekly diesel-powered freight on the Waltham Sub.) At 3:50 P.M. the little train got under way.

Afraid of getting hung up in traffic on the streets of a city completely new to us, we headed ten miles out of town to Aylmer, where we caught the 425 running through a tunnel of trees. Aylmer was one of just three firm intermediate stops en route to Waltham; at the modest open shelter there, a handful of neatly uniformed schoolgirls piled off the coach, heading home after a day at an Ottawa private school. From there on the train led us on a merry chase. With just a handful of passengers aboard, the D4g breezed through most of the conditional stops with nothing more than a whistle and a wave.

The sun was just setting when the mixed arrived at Campbell's Bay, on Chenal Grand Calumet, a channel of the Ottawa River

Evening water stop at Campbell's Bay (all).

All photos: Roger Cook

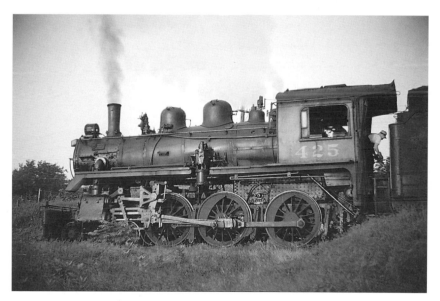

that formed Calumet Island. After stopping at the station to do some head-end work, the 425 moved up to a red octagonal water tank, located right on the shore of the channel. The fireman hauled down the spout, completing an exquisite picture of branch-line railroading: panting locomotive glowing in the last rays of golden sun; clapboard tank of ancient design, crowned by a ball float that lent assurance of the tank's fullness; the smell of water and of the dry grasses of early fall, overlaid with the steam locomotive's characteristic odors.

Diesel-powered Mixed for Kincardine backs to the wye at Palmerston.

Jim Shaughnessy

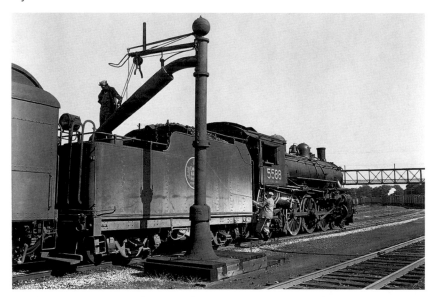

No. 5588 takes water before its Palmerston stop.

Don Wood

It was nearly full dark by the time the train reached Waltham, where we rode with the crew as they wyed the train, then grabbed a bite to eat and found a modest motel in nearby Fort Coulonge for the night. The next morning we were back at "the Bay" as Ottawa-bound 425 shuffled up to the tank in the very different, much softer post-dawn light, brightening as the sun broke through the clouds.

That lovely, still morning at Campbell's Bay was bittersweet. For us, the diminutive Ten-Wheeler, classic two-car train, and octagonal water tank epitomized Canadian branch-line and secondary main-line railroading, and we sensed we'd now seen our allotted portion of that evocative mix. As we followed No. 425 back toward Ottawa on now-familiar ground, we regretted that we'd been born just a few years too late—the lament of countless other rail enthusiasts of every generation.

We regretted that we'd never experience first-hand, as Bob Collins and other photographers had, those New Brunswick 4-4-0's. We knew we'd not follow in the footsteps of Don Wood as he chased Moguls and Ten-Wheelers on Ontario branch lines or stand on the iron footbridge at Palmerston with Jim Shaughnessy as he observed the action below. In fact, CNR's branch lines radiating from Palmerston had gone diesel just a week or so after our Toronto trip the previous April, and we assumed CPR's Ontario steam was all but gone as well.

So Campbell's Bay, with its perfect combination of bucolic setting and branch-line appurtenances, and No. 425 with its little train would have to suffice for us. And less than a month after our visit, "that wretched little engine" was gone, too, its fires dropped for good. In another month, the train itself was history.

Train M329, the Southampton mixed, gets orders from the Harriston operator before leaving the Owen Sound Subdivision at Harriston Junction.

Jim Shaughnessy

Palmerston was the operating hub of a network of branch lines radiating to Owen Sound, Durham, Southampton, and Kincardine. Its two-story wooden station abutted two legs of a wye where the main lines from Guelph and Stratford met, and an iron footbridge over the modest yard provided an unobstructed view of the squat wooden roundhouse and engine-servicing facilities. "Trains would literally explode out of Palmerston in all directions," photographer Jim Shaughnessy recalls. "There was always something happening, and you just couldn't chase all the trains. It was like the late 1920's compared to Toronto, a real time warp with lots of smaller power on leisurely schedules." One of these trains, No. 179 for Southampton (left), is ready for its 9:10 departure. Facing page, top: Pacific 5548 must depart with the Owen Sound train before Ten-Wheeler 1348 can back on to the baggage car and two coaches for Southampton. Facing page, bottom: August 1, 1957, at the Palmerston roundhouse.

All photos: Jim Shaughnessy

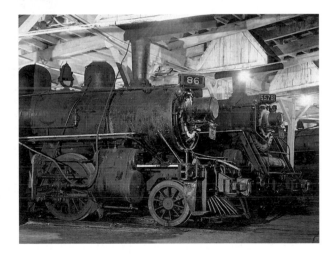

Way freight from Owen Sound at Tara, July 1957.

A 1957 Dodge meets a 1910 Mogul at Chesley.

Dodge in a Ditch

In July 1957, John Rehor and I were shooting branch-line operations out of Allandale, Ontario. In particular, we were after the way freight to Meaford, a tiny town on Georgian Bay. Driving my car—a 1957 Dodge D-500, one of those swept-wing beauties with spinning hubcaps and dual antennas—we caught up with the train, powered that day by a little Ten-Wheeler, halfway up the branch at

Elmvale. After hightailing it out of town to get ahead of him, we swung onto a dirt road that paralleled the tracks. In a rush, I pulled off the road and into a big drainage ditch, which I couldn't see because it was all covered with brush. The car nosed in, with the right rear wheel up in the air—no traction at all.

Well, we thought, we might as well get this shot, because it's probably going to be the last one of the day. The train came and went, leaving an empty silence. Just as we were trying to figure out what to do next, we heard

this "putt-putt-putt-putt-putt" from down the line, and here came a little gas car loaded with half a dozen French-Canadian gandy dancers. We flagged them down.

"We've got a problem," we said, and pointed, since our verbal communication was limited. The track workers, big, burly guys, got off the section speeder and came over to survey the situation. They took one look at the car, saw our plight, and lifted the Dodge right out of the ditch as if they were picking up the evening paper from the front steps. We thanked them and, without much ado, they climbed back on the speeder and were on their way in a roar of unmuffled exhaust.

What an unlikely situation! That a two-trains-a-week branch would be operated, let alone maintained, and then these guys happening along at just the right time. It was harrowing, I'll tell you that, out in the middle of nowhere. I don't know what we would have done if that speeder hadn't come along—but good things always seemed to happen around Canadian rails.

—Don Wood

All photos: Don Wood

On a return visit in July 1958, photographers Wood and Rehor encountered the "up" way freight from Palmerston to Owen Sound. Fireman Norman Bowes recognized them and (top right) is having some fun dangling from the cab of Ten-Wheeler 1530, a former Canadian Northern locomotive. Both it and the former Grand Trunk Mogul they had seen the previous year were built in 1910. Bottom right: Ten-Wheeler and Bowes are at Harriston.

In September 1958, Sharbot Lake, Ontario, still retained some semblance of its former importance as a junction where CPR's original Montreal–Toronto main was crossed by the Kingston Subdivision, which connected Kingston on the Lake Ontario Shore main line with Renfrew on the Montreal–Sudbury transcontinental main. Facing page: Train M782 has arrived from Renfrew, while D10 No. 1087—which has run light from Smiths Falls—waits to trade places with No. 840 for the return trip. Between M782's arrival at 1 P.M. and its departure at 2:40 as M783, passenger trains 35 from Montreal and 36 from Toronto will have paused to make connections. After both passenger trains and the mixed have cleared, No. 840 (seen at left taking water) will run to Smiths Falls, and G1 Pacific 2224 will follow it with a way freight (below).

All photos: Don Wood

All photos: Don Wood

Pacific 5257 with Uxbridge Subdivision Train 94 from Toronto to Belleville (above) slows for water at Blackwater, Ontario. Earlier in the day, Pacific 5589 (right top and bottom) arrived on the branch-line freight from Coboconk.

The Lindsay–Belleville way freight on the Campbellford Subdivision in July 1958.

Steam operations lasted on CPR subsidiary Quebec Central Railway until March 1960. Vallée Jonction was the center of activity, for its roundhouse dispatched steam for way-freight assignments on the Quebec Subdivision main line and mixed trains on the 79-mile Chaudière Subdivision to Lac Frontière and the 60-mile Mégantic Subdivision from Tring Junction to Mégantic. In May 1959, CPR D10 Ten-Wheeler 1039 arrives with the mixed from Lac Frontière (above), and baggage is unloaded from the combine (right). After switching its train, 1039 takes on water at the roundhouse (facing page, left). Shortly after the Dayliner from Quebec has left for Sherbrooke, the mixed train for Mégantic (facing page, right) hustles across the Chaudière River bridge. It will follow the Dayliner's route ten miles south to Tring Junction and then branch off toward its destination.

Quebec Central-lettered D10 No.1083 leads a southbound way freight along Lac Aylmer, near Disraeli.

All photos: Jim Shaughnessy

STEAM IN SNOW

Who would argue that steam locomotives in snow generate a special magic? It's an aura of beauty and adversity all at once. Perhaps this magic stems from the collision of opposites, the juxtaposition of fire and ice. Add in the I-think-I-can drama of machinery asked to perform in difficult conditions. Or maybe what's special is largely visual: the blanketing snow that removes background clutter and leaves images with the elegant simplicity of Oriental watercolors; the billowing steam that envelopes running gear or, intermixed with coal smoke that turns it gray, piles high above a laboring locomotive.

In any case, no less an aesthete than Walt Whitman—the noted American poet of the latter nineteenth century, when railroads were entering their heyday—saw its beauty, which he captured in "To a Locomotive in Winter."

"Thee in the driving storm even as now," he wrote in his ode to steam, "the snow, the winter-day declining,/Thee in thy panoply, thy measured dual throbbing and thy beat convulsive . . ./Thy ponderous side-bars, parallel and connecting rods, gyrating, shuttling at thy sides . . . ."

No poets we, but beauty of that sort was on our minds in December 1959, a few days after Christmas, when—with Steve Ward, a neighborhood friend and fellow steam aficionado—we headed north once again to Montreal, intent on capturing on film the greatest remaining steam-in-snow show in North America. By now we were traveling by automobile, so we had thought about branching out and heading for the hinterlands. To that end, we'd made inquiries, and in due course had heard from R. B. Scott, superintendent of motive power and rolling stock for CPR's Atlantic Region.

"Referring to your letter of November 11th, requesting certain information on steam power operating in and around Vallee Junction, Megantic and Lac Frontier," he'd written, "at the present time there are only four locomotives operating in the area mentioned and there are only about two engines dispatched per day." This we thought to be slim pickings, so we returned to what was then the mother lode of Canadian steam: Montreal, with its reliable diet of CPR Pacifics and Hudsons in suburban service, where diesels had made few inroads. (On the other hand, Canadian National by then was effectively dieselized in the East.)

Canada is, of course, famous for its winters, so we weren't surprised to encounter some on our visit. Though prepared for snow, we hadn't fully anticipated the brevity of December daylight at roughly 45 degrees north latitude, where Montreal sits. The outbound, evening commuter rush was fully after dark, while the inbound rush was in the gray light of early morning, particularly when the sky was socked in and leaking snow.

Turcot.
Jim Shaughnessy

It is ten degrees below zero at Sutton, Quebec, and two locomotives are tied up there on this frigid December night. D10 No. 970 and a combination baggage-coach have arrived from Waterloo, and before they leave the station the crew loads the engine's pilot with firewood for the bunkhouse stove. Jubilee 2927 is off the commuter run from Montreal and will return there the next day, departing before the sun is up.

All photos: Jim Shaughnessy

Pacific 5293 on CNR's Train 23 at Sherbrooke is about to leave for Montreal (all).

All photos: Jim Shaughnessy

Action at Lennoxville, Quebec: Left, an eastbound extra with P2 Mikado 5396 passes the station. Above, CPR's doubledheaded Extra 5329 West will pick up orders from the tower operator before it bangs over the diamond crossing with CNR's line to Island Pond, Vermont, and Portland, Maine. Facing page: The trailing engine's fireman waves to the photographer as a G2 Pacific and P2 Mikado storm past the station to build momentum for the eastbound climb out of the Massawippi River valley.

All photos: Jim Shaughnessy

Clouds of billowing smoke marked the passage of westbound (below) and eastbound (right) doubleheaders at the Massawippi River bridge just east of Lennoxville.

All photos: Jim Shaughnessy

Eastbound freight near Cookshire.

All photos: Jim Shaughnessy

Facing page and left: A westbound slows to pick up orders at Cookshire, then departs past a team of horses while their driver loads coal from a hopper car. Above: P2 Mikes off an eastbound grain train are spotted for water at Cookshire.

Eastbound way freight at Milan.

All photos: Karl Zimmermann

ready to work east to Mégantic, the next division point.

Under gray skies 2663 set out with just an l.c.l. boxcar (worked at numerous stops along the way) and scale test car ahead of the caboose. She arrived at Mégantic about the same time that the "Scoot"—the triweekly mixed train from Brownville Junction, Maine—pulled in behind Mikado No. 5107 (built in CPR's Angus Shops). No. 3514 was busy working the yard there; this Baldwin-built 2-8-0 had been fired up because the Alco diesel switcher that usually drew the assignment had been pressed into service on a snowplow extra.

Shooting its comings and goings, we bumped into David Plowden, a photographer whose eloquent work we admired even then. He'd ridden the "Scoot" from Brownville Junction and would return the next day, which he surmised would be the final trip in steam. That night we had a hearty supper in the dining room of the Queen's Hotel, then lay in bed listening to the sounds of whistling and slack running in as 3514 butted cars around the yard.

When the "Scoot" left town at 7:30 the next morning for its run over CPR's International of Maine route, carrying the markers was open-platform observation *Fort Simpson* serving as pay car, an institution even more outmoded than the steam locomotive on the other end. Once a week, paymaster (and rail author) Omer Lavallée traversed this remote line, doling out wages in cash to employees, who presented themselves in person aboard the pay car. (This was the last pay car to run in North America; it would be retired about three months later.)

We headed west, following 2663 to Sherbrooke on a dazzling blue-sky morning as the Pacific rolled a goodly string of boxcars across a snow-covered landscape. At Cookshire, the Pacific grabbed its caboose and, pushing a wedge plow, headed down the

The "Scoot" leaves Mégantic behind steam for the last time (both).

6.7-mile branch to Sawyerville (formerly owned by Maine Central), returning with a single boxcar in tow. We drove on to Farnham, where we were disappointed to find the Ten-Wheeler off the way freight from Sherbrooke—No. 1072, with smokebox-centered headlight and "Quebec Central" spread across its tender—already in the roundhouse with it fires banked. (No. 1072 had been built in 1912 in Schenectady by Alco for use on CPR's Vermont lines. The 4-6-0 had been borrowed, but never owned, by Quebec Central.)

Disappointment deepened when the night roundhouse foreman explained that 1072 was going out of service—that, in fact, in the next morning's pre-dawn hours, a diesel would head east with the Sherbrooke way freight. No doubt our chagrin was apparent to the foreman, since before long the hostler was lining the turntable to exhume the Ten-Wheeler. Steam pressure was dying as he backed the 1072 onto the turntable, posed it there for photos, then left it next to the roundhouse, where we continued popping away at it with No. 25 flashbulbs.

Then the foreman explained further about the next morning's way freight. The unit in question was actually headed out to

The "Scoot" arrives at Mégantic.

Mégantic yard's west end.   *All photos: Karl Zimmermann*

Switching out a snowplow from the "Scoot's" consist.

dieselize the Drummondville Subdivision. At Foster, he said, there would be an engine swap, with No. 946 (which we'd seen a few days before locked in the enginehouse at Drummondville) coming off the branch and taking over the Sherbrooke job. We didn't ask what class of diesel it would be, and didn't care.

The next morning we awoke with a start—and then a sick feeling in our stomachs. We'd overslept, and No. 946, by now on the way freight for Sherbrooke, surely would be far ahead of us. It was. Scrambling in hot pursuit, we caught the train switching at Magog, with snow-covered Lake Memphrémagog as backdrop. Once the 946 was tied up at Sherbrooke, we hightailed it to Mégantic to photograph the arrival of the "Scoot."

Mégantic switcher.

When it pulled in behind an RS3 we were crestfallen. Plowden had been right. We didn't even bother to take a picture. So the day before, it seemed, on March 29, we'd witnessed the end of steam on the Brownville Junction mixed. That meant we'd also seen the last steam-hauled, regularly scheduled passenger service to run in the United States, since steam had been retired from Grand Trunk Western's Detroit-Durand locals—generally considered the last passenger steam in the U. S.—two days earlier.

We were up in timely fashion the next morning to follow No. 946 as it worked back from Sherbrooke to Farnham. Fields were still ankle-deep in snow, but the warmth of spring was in the air this misty morning. West of Magog, where the tracks make a broad, sweeping climb toward Mount Orford, the snow breathed

fog. The 946 whistled in the distance, then materialized out of the shrouded evergreens, clanking around the curve under its own gray-white cloud, trailing a short train of mixed freight in boxcars and gondolas.

The next day, crisp and cloudless, we would follow Pacific No. 2229 peddling its goods from Farnham to Montreal's St. Luc Yard. But somehow we had said farewell to Canadian steam the day before near Mount Orford, as the ghostly Ten-Wheeler charged upgrade out of the mist, whistling plaintively for the road crossing, its modest train clattering behind.

And now, almost forty years later, the Form 19 still rustles as we pass it back and forth. "Eng 946 run Extra . . ." That it did, for the last time, on March 31, 1960.

G5 Pacific 1201 leads Farnham–Montreal local past South Junction tower approaching Montreal West, March 1960.

At Cookshire, No. 2663 prepares to plow out the branch to Sawyerville.

All photos: Karl Zimmermann

Baldwin Locomotive Works built M4g Consolidation 3514 in May 1907. Two months short of its fifty-third birthday, it switches Mégantic yard for possibly the last time, its grim-faced engineer no doubt aware of the veteran locomotive's impending demise.

No. 1201 completes its run at Farnham.

Roger Cook

On the turntable at Farnham.

Roger Cook

No. 1072 under steam for the last time.

Karl Zimmermann

On April 1, 1960, the golden glow of the setting sun helps disguise the grime that has begun to accumulate on these locomotives congregating at St. Luc, location of CPR's most modern hump yard and an impressive brick roundhouse and diesel repair shop. The previous December the roundhouse leads had been full of steaming locomotives, but by April Consolidation 3638, Royal Hudson 2841, standard Hudson 2811, and G1 Pacific 2229 were among the last survivors under steam, and soon they too would be cold.

All photos: Karl Zimmermann

138

Pop-Pop, Trout, and Brownville Junction

To my grandfather, fly-fishing was tantamount to a religion and the trout and landlocked salmon of northern Maine amounted to nirvana. Every summer the lakes and streams of Piscataquis County produced their siren call and, like it or not, the family made a pilgrimage to some remote cabin on a lake. The usual path to this paradise was U.S. Route 1 to Route 2, then 157 into Millinocket.

For me, steam locomotives held the same fascination that trout did for Pop-Pop.

Both photos: Steve Ward

It was the mid 1950's, and I knew that both the Maine Central (which we followed for a stretch) and the Bangor & Aroostook (which we crossed) had dieselized. But when we stopped at Mattawamkeag for lunch I might see steam on the Canadian Pacific's International of Maine Division.

On this particular trip, however, Pop took Route 11 north, which bisected the CPR at Brownville Junction. I had no idea that Brownville Junction was a division point, and we would no doubt have driven right through had I not seen No. 3519, a Consolidation (an M4g, I would learn later, built in 1907) shoving a cut of cars over the bridge that crossed Route 11 and the Pleasant River.

Somehow I convinced Pop to turn up a cinder drive that lead to a compact yard and engine terminal, complete with timber coal chute and a two-story, wood-frame railroad YMCA. All this to take in, and Pop said I had just 30 minutes to do it. He wanted to be sure we got to "camp" by supper. Happily, though, everything seemed to fall into place during that half hour. G2s Pacific No. 2584 came in for servicing off the "Scoot" from Mégantic at the same time that 3519 was tying up. A couple of Mikados stood outside the brick roundhouse, and there were several more inside, along with a dead D10 4-6-0.

Most Downeast railroaders are fishermen, so Pop had cornered the hostler and gotten the latest scoop on what the trout were taking on the West Branch of the Penobscot while I shot my pictures.

With some help from the CPR, Pop-Pop provided my half hour of nirvana.

—*Steve Ward*

Steve Ward

Both photos: Jim Shaughnessy

On Easter break from college, Jim Shaughnessy drove all day from Troy, New York, to Brownville Junction, where he met his friend Sandy Worthen, who arrived that night on the *Atlantic Limited* from Montreal. They spent several days photographing steam trains near the yard, venturing beyond there only once, on a round trip on the "Scoot" to Onawa. Jim Britt, one of the Brownville dispatchers, arranged for the eastbound to pick them up at Ship Pond Stream Viaduct after they hiked back there from the westbound's Onawa stop. Above left, the eastbound "Scoot" crosses the viaduct. Above right: Britt at his desk.

P2 Mikado 5415 pulls out of Brownville Junction with westbound tonnage, while the yard switcher classifies Bangor and Aroostook interchange traffic (left). Later, while Ten-Wheeler 1075 (reassigned to Brownville after CPR's lines in Vermont were dieselized) continues sorting carloads of Maine potatoes, the "Scoot" departs behind G2 Pacific 2584 (above). At the opposite end of the yard, doubleheaded P1 Mikes are reflected in the Pleasant River as they depart for McAdam, New Brunswick, with a train for the port of Saint John (facing page).

All photos: Jim Shaughnessy

STEAM LIVES ON

Within a month after we'd photographed Engine 946 climbing out of the fog at Mount Orford, CPR and CNR revenue steam was virtually gone. April 1960 was a time of last runs: in New Brunswick, steam ended on the fourteenth, when CPR D10 No. 986 dropped its fires at McAdam after returning there from St. Stephen; on the twenty-fifth, Mountain 6043 arrived at Winnipeg on Train 76 from The Pas with the last scheduled steam run anywhere on CNR; and on the thirtieth CPR 2-8-0 No. 3722 crossed Great Hog Bay Trestle for the last time on a Port McNicoll–Orillia round trip that marked the end of steam on CPR's Ontario branch lines.

That same day, CPR 4-4-0 No. 136, recently retired from Chipman–Norton standby duty, doubleheaded with D10 No. 815 on a Toronto–Cooksville excursion—a trip that was just a preview of the next day's feature attraction. On May 1, 136 and 815 were joined by 1057, another D10, for a spectacular and widely witnessed tripleheaded excursion from Toronto up through the Forks of Credit to Orangeville. Years later, Frank Bunker (with whom Jim Shaughnessy had ridden to Orr's Lake), who fired one of the locomotives that day, remembered their arrival at Orangeville.

"You couldn't see the ground for the people," he said. "It was just like a human sea." Two weeks earlier, excursions had run on CPR out of Montreal: to Mount Orford behind G5 No. 1201

Great Hog Bay Trestle, April 30, 1960.

on April 16, and the next day to Smiths Falls with Hudson 2811. On June 5, Royal Hudson 2857 made its last run when it retraced the route of the "boat train" on a Toronto to Port McNicoll excursion.

Regularly assigned steam lingered in Montreal's Lakeshore commuter service until June, when finally there were enough diesels to kill the last fires. Not all the locomotives were retired, however. A few were carefully lubricated and prepared for storage in case they would be needed during the next winter's annual

Tripleheader excursion at Snelgrove, returning to Toronto, May 1, 1960.
Both photos: Don Wood

motive-power crunch. Although none ever turned a wheel in revenue service, some were fired up at St. Luc around Christmas 1960 (but never used) and again for a few weeks from late February to early March 1961, when they provided steam heat for passenger cars while the Glen coach yard's heating system was being repaired. Though coaled at The Glen, they returned to St. Luc for other servicing and boiler washes, moving under their own steam between the two locations and thus offering one last chance to see CPR steam (albeit running light) in company service.

Particularly on CNR, main-line excursion steam remained active for several decades past the official "last" steam runs: CNR's were on September 3 and 4, 1960, with Northern 6153 on

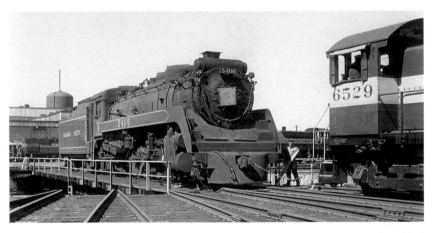

Steve Ward

Shop laborers have capped the stack, boxed the headlight, and liberally oiled driver boxes and tender journals of P2 Mikado 5406. Now a Montreal Locomotive Works diesel will stretch the cable attached to the 2-8-2's coupler and ease the engine off the turntable and onto a roundhouse track. Once the switcher has pulled the Mikado clear of the table, it will get behind and push it into the roundhouse. It's September 5, 1960, and nine steamers are being prepared for storage here at St. Luc.

Montreal–Joliette and Montreal–Ottawa round trips, and CPR's November 6, with 4-4-0 No. 29 on a St. Lin Subdivision excursion, which also commemorated the seventy-fifth anniversary of the driving of the last spike at Craigellachie. Even before this 6153 trip, sister 6167 was operating in excursion service, mainly in the Toronto area. This Northern would remain active through September 26 and 27, 1964, when it would doublehead on two excursions out of Toronto with its replacement, Northern 6218 (which had been the last steam locomotive outshopped at Stratford, in November 1963). The 6153 continued in occasional excursion service out of Montreal; in 1962 it had teamed up with Pacific 5107 for several trips before both were retired.

Although No. 6218 ran mainly on excursions from Toronto and Montreal, it also traveled to New London, Connecticut, Portland, Maine, and Chicago. When it was retired on July 4, 1971, it seemed that CNR's steam program had finally ended.

Loss turned to anticipation in July 1972, however, when oil-fired Mountain 6060 moved east from Jasper, where it had been on display at the station. (In trade, Jasper got Mountain 6015 from Canadian Railroad Historical Association's St. Constant museum.) Although 6060's distinctive cone nose had been removed in the 1950's after its transfer to Western service, Montreal's Pointe St. Charles Shops fabricated a new one during a leisurely year-long overhaul. No. 6060 emerged as a "Bullet-Nosed Betty" once again, resurrected for a second life.

CNR operated 6060 for almost seven years, from September 1973 until July 1980, including regularly scheduled Toronto–Niagara Falls "Steam Specials" from June to September that were listed in the 1976 and 1977 system timetables as Train 6060. In 1978, VIA Rail Canada and CNR jointly operated the specials on Wednesdays and Saturdays from July 1 to September 2. With

While photographing the last of Quebec Central steam at Vallée Jonction in early March of 1960, Bob Collins learned that the Chipman–Norton branch's diesel-hydraulic unit had broken down. Hoping to reach New Brunswick before repairs could be completed, he headed east, and on March 5 he found No. 29 with Train M559 crossing the recently rebuilt trestle at Pennlyn (below) and arriving at Chipman (left).

Both photos: Robert F. Collins

Lambton roundhouse, May 1, 1960.

All photos: Don Wood

6060, CNR's multifarious steam program finally came to an end. (However, 6060's excursion life did not; it was purchased by the Province of Alberta and moved West for further operation.)

Though CPR's November 1960 excursion with No. 29 was the last official steam run, it wasn't the end of steam on CPR rails. In the 1970's, Nos. 136 and 1057, by then both privately owned, made trips out of Toronto sponsored by the Ontario Rail Association—most memorably, when they doubleheaded to Owen Sound on two-day October trips from 1973 to 1975. Prior to the first of these, No. 136 had been shopped and backdated to an 1880's look for use in "The National Dream," a 1973

Canadian Broadcasting Company documentary about building the Canadian Pacific Railway across Canada and the unifying political effect of its completion.

Also in 1973, Pacific No. 1201, which had been on display at Ottawa's National Museum of Science and Technology, was sent to John Street roundhouse in Toronto to be rebuilt by Ontario Rail Association members. The museum had contracted with CPR to use 18 miles of its Maniwaki Branch, to Wakefield, for regular weekly steam excursions from July to October. Since it took some time to ready 1201, Ontario Rail's 1057 was used for the 1974 and 1975 seasons. The 1201 made its first test run on

June 7, 1976, and took over excursion duties that year, continuing for an even ten seasons. Maniwaki, Barry's Bay, and Montreal were among 1201's periodic off-line destinations, but its most ambitious moves were transcontinental.

No. 1201's last Wakefield trip was on September 1, 1985. Soon afterward, a diesel ferried the Pacific and three museum cars west to participate in CPR's Last Spike Centennial Celebration. On the morning of November 7, now without diesel assist, 1201 headed a six-car passenger consist from Revelstoke to Craigellachie and return; following the festivities, a diesel hauled 1201 to Vancouver where, after spending the winter in storage, the Pacific would participate in Steam Expo at the Expo 86 World's Fair, which had dual themes of transportation and communications.

On May 23, 1986, almost one hundred years after CPR's first transcontinental train had reached Port Moody (now part of Vancouver), Steam Expo began with the Grand Parade of Steam. Former CPR Royal Hudson 2860, now province-owned and regularly assigned to BC Rail's North Vancouver–Squamish excursion train, led a procession of 17 locomotives, with 1201 the last in line. (No. 6060 had been scheduled to bring up the rear but arrived a few days late from Alberta, where it had just completed a major overhaul.) While 2860 was at Steam Expo, Consolidation 3716, also ex-CPR, substituted on the tourist runs. No. 1201 returned East in July after attending the centennial celebration commemorating CPR's arrival at Port Moody. Although again paired with a diesel for most of the trip, at Field 1201 dropped its helper and, with just its three-car train, proceeded upgrade through the Spiral Tunnels to Lake Louise and Calgary.

The Atlantic coast was 1201's destination in June 1989, when it moved eastbound with a diesel to help commemorate the International of Maine Division's opening for through traffic a

Approaching Orangeville, May 1, 1960 (both).

century earlier. That line east of Sherbrooke was then operated by CPR subsidiary Canadian Atlantic Railway, which permitted steam-only operation east of Megantic —a replicated "Scoot" mixed-train consist of one freshly painted CAR red boxcar together with coaches, a yellow CPR van, and a business car.

Belleville, Ontario.   *Roger Cook*

Nineteen eighty-nine was a special year for New Brunswick steam events. After 1201 operated from both Saint John and McAdam on well-publicized public excursions, a very low-profile charter—just CPR 4-4-0 No. 29 and one coach—ran near Moncton September 24 on the Salem & Hillsborough tourist railway. In conjunction with the charter, the prior day's regular train was CNR light Ten-Wheeler No. 1009, a baggage car, and coaches—all in CNR green livery. The 29 and two coaches handled regular service on charter day.

Just five years later, on September 16, 1994, an early morning fire, suspected to be arson, destroyed the line's maintenance shop and office; most of the equipment stored inside and nearby— including two diesels, three passenger cars, two freight cars, shop equipment, and spare parts—was a total loss. No. 1009 was outside and not badly damaged, but the flaming roof collapsed around No. 29, which had been stored indoors. It never ran again but was cosmetically restored in 1996 and sent west to Calgary for display outside Canadian Pacific's new headquarters.

Except for CPR Hudsons 2811 and 2857 and Ten-Wheeler

815, none of the excursion engines were scrapped. Northern 6153 is at the CRHA museum in St. Constant. No. 6167 is displayed in Guelph, and 6218, coupled to a wooden caboose decked out in Morency orange and maple leaf herald, is at the Fort Erie Railroad Museum. CNR Pacific 5107 is at Kapuskasing, while CPR 1201 is out of service and stored at the museum in Ottawa.

CNR Ten-Wheeler 1009 on the Salem & Hillsborough in New Brunswick, as well as CPR 136 and 1057, now operating in Ontario on the South Simcoe Railway (part of the former CNR Hamilton-Allandale line and headquartered at Tottenham), remain to carry on a long tradition of branch-line steam railway operations.

For the present, main-line steam runs only in the West: 6060 on occasional outings and former CPR Royal Hudson 2860 and Consolidation 3716 on BC Rail. Wouldn't it be nice if 2816, again CPR property, could join them and be illuminated once more by popping flashbulbs?

Watering 6153 and 5107, Cantic, Quebec.   *Jim Shaughnessy*

150

Turcot roundhouse.

Turcot West, September 3, 1960.

Returning from Joliette, September 3, 1960.

All photos: Roger Cook

No. 6167 on a westbound excursion at Mariposa, Ontario.

Roger Cook

CPR's last steam crew.

Photo runby on the St. Lin Subdivision, November 6, 1960.

Both photos: Karl Zimmermann

No. 136 has cut off (top left), and engineer Frank Bunker watches from its cab as 1057 lugs Ontario Rail's October 12, 1974, excursion into Owen Sound. Botton left, the excursion returns to Toronto the following day.

All photos: Roger Cook

On the Salem & Hillsborough, No. 1009 crosses a tributary of the Petitcodiac River at low tide.

All photos: Roger Cook

G5 No. 1201, the last locomotive ever built at CPR's Angus Shops, kept the steam flame burning in the 1970's and '80's. Top left: Passing log booms in the Gatineau River near Chelsea, the Pacific heads back to Ottawa with a Wakefield excursion. Bottom left: Ralph Humphries and Earl Roberts are among the Bytown Railway Society volunteer crew who readied the Pacific for weekend operations. Facing page: Jacques Beaubien Jr.'s 1939 Dodge touring sedan waits as 1201 executes a photo runby on an excursion to Maniwaki, Quebec.

Although our names appear there as co-authors, we are privileged to share this book's title page with Jim Shaughnessy and Don Wood, gifted photographers who traveled extensively in search of Canadian steam and who shared their negative files and memories with us. Without their involvement, this volume would have been far poorer in both scope and artistry.

Roger Cook

Bob Collins and Steve Ward were also generous contributors. A good friend since childhood and a frequent traveling companion, Steve not only supplied photographs and vivid recollections but also loaned books and timetables. Most important of all, he was a constant source of encouragement and advice. Vincent Alvino was another congenial fellow traveler on our early trips. Earl Roberts, also an old friend, currently edits Bytown Railway Society's *Branchline* and co-edits its *Canadian Trackside Guide*; he helped us get our facts in order and encouraged our efforts. Greg McDonnell, a new friend, supported and helped shape the project.

Our parents trusted us to act as responsible adults and saw our teenage travels in search of steam as a potentially broadening (if sometimes puzzling) educational experience. Without their trust and encouragement, and the current support of our families and friends, there would have been no book.

—Roger Cook and Karl Zimmermann
Oradell, New Jersey, April 1999

Andreae, Christopher. *Lines of Country: An Atlas of Railway and Waterway History in Canada.* Erin, Ontario: The Boston Mills Press, 1997.

Beaudette, Edward H. *Central Vermont Railway.* Newton, New Jersey: Carstens Publications, Inc., 1982.

Beaumont, Ralph. *Steam Trains to the Bruce.* Cheltenham, Ontario: The Boston Mills Press, 1977.

Bowers, Peter. *Two Divisions to Bluewater.* Erin, Ontario: The Boston Mills Press, 1983.

Boyd, Jim. "SteamEXPO and the Grand Parade," *Railfan & Railroad,* VI (September 1986), 32-38.

Clegg, Anthony and Corley, Ray. *Canadian National Steam Power.* Montreal: Trains and Trolleys, 1969.

"CN/CP Steam on the Move-1959" (video). Toronto: Village Station Productions, Inc., 1998.

Dean, Murray W. and Hanna, David B. *Canadian Pacific Diesel Locomotives.* Toronto: Railfare Enterprises Limited, 1981.

Donaldson, Ian. *Enter Diesel-Exit Steam.* Calgary: The British Railway Modellers of North America, 1994.

Dorin, Patrick C. *Canadian Pacific Railway.* Seattle: Superior Publishing Company, 1974.

DuFresne, Duncan. "The 'Pontiac' Revisited," *Branchline,* XXX (February 1991), 13-19.

"The Final Chapter: CPR Steam in Ontario" (video). Schomberg, Ontario: Rail Innovations, n.d.

Hansen, Keith, M. A. *Last Train from Lindsay.* Roseneath, Ontario: Sandy Flats Publications, 1997.

Hart, George M. *Letter in Steam Locomotive,* I (December 1959), 2.

Ingles, J. David. "Again-Two Plain Iron Spikes," *Trains,* XLVI (February 1986), 18B-19.

Ingles, J. David ed. "Expo: 10 Days of Steam, Smoke, Whistles, and Bells," *Trains,* XLVI (September 1986), 18-21.

Jago, Philip B. "From Pacific to Atlantic," *Branchline,* XXVIII (July-August 1989), 7-8.

_____. "Never Say Die," *Branchline,* XXVIII (July-August 1989), 11-19.

Lavallée, Omer. *Canadian Pacific in the East (Volume One),* Calgary: The British Railway Modellers of North America, 1984.

_____. *Canadian Pacific in the East (Volume Two),* Calgary: The British Railway Modellers of North America, 1989.

_____. *Canadian Pacific Steam Locomotives.* Toronto: Railfare Enterprises Limited, 1985.

_____. "Pay Car on the International of Maine," *Canadian Rail,* (January 1966), 3-20.

_____. "1201's Eastern Odyssey-The Route," *Branchline,* XXVIII (July-August 1989), 8-10.

Lowe, J. Norman. *Canadian National in the East (Volume One).* Calgary: The British Railway Modellers of North America, 1981.

_____. *Canadian National in the East (Volume Two).* Calgary: The British Railway Modellers of North America, 1983.

MacKay, Donald and Perry, Lorne. *Train Country.* Forest Park, Illinois: Heimburger House Publishing Company, 1995.

Morgan, David P. ed. *Canadian Steam!* Milwaukee: Kalmbach Publishing Company, 1961.

Panko, Andrew and Bowen, Peter. *Steam in Niagara.* Fonthill, Ontario: Niagara Rail Publications, 1983.

Paterson, Allan and George, Dick. *Steam at Oakville: A Day on the Oakville Subdivision.* Erin, Ontario: The Boston Mills Press, 1988.

Riddell, John. *The Railways of Toronto: The First Hundred Years.* Calgary: The British Railway Modellers of North America, 1991.

_____. *The Railways of Toronto (Volume Two).* Calgary: The British Railway Modellers of North America, 1994.

Ritchie, Ronald S. *Canadian Pacific's Montreal Lakeshore Commuter Services (Volume One),* Calgary: The British Railway Modellers of North America, 1990.

Roberts, Earl. "Apologize for What?" *Branchline,* XXXIII (November 1994), 10-11.

Rossiter, W. H. N. *Canadian Pacific in Southern Ontario (Volume One),* Calgary: The British Railway Modellers of North America, 1981.

_____. *Canadian Pacific in Southern Ontario (Volume Two),* Calgary: The British Railway Modellers of North America, 1983.

_____. *Canadian Pacific in Southern Ontario (Volume Three),* Calgary: The British Railway Modellers of North America, 1986.

Shaughnessy, Jim. "The Winter Show at Cookshire," *Railfan & Railroad,* VIII (February 1989), 33-40.

"Steam Memories of Ontario" (video). Schomberg, Ontario: Rail Innovations, n.d.

Wilson, Ian. *Steam in Allandale: The Story of a CNR Division Point in the 1950's.* Orillia, Ontario: Canadian Branchline Miniatures, 1998.

Wood, Don. *Locomotives in My Life.* Earlton, New York: Audio-Visual Designs, 1974.

Young, William S. "Those C.P.R. 4-4-0's," *Steam Locomotive,* I (October 1959), 4-10.

Branchline (various issues)

The Official Guide of the Railways (various issues)

Railfan & Railroad (various issues)

Steam Locomotive (various issues)

Trains (various issues)